These Last Days

These Last Days

ANGELIC MESSENGERS REVEAL THE FUTURE

Dottie Mae Goard

Hope Publishing House
Pasadena, California

Scriptures quoted are from the *New Revised Standard Version Bible,* copyright © 1989 by the Division of Christian Education of the National Council of the Churches of Christ in the United States of America, used by permission. Excerpts from "Valediction" are reprinted from *Selected Poems, 1969-1981* by Richard Shelton, used by permission of the University of Pittsburgh Press, © 1982 by Richard Shelton; from "Be Thou My Vision" Alt. © 1989 The United Methodist Publishing House, used by permission from *The United Methodist Hymnal;from* "Through It All" by Andrae Crouch, copyright © 1971 by Manna Music, Inc., used by permission; from "How Great Thou Art" by Stuart K. Hine, copyright © 1953, renewed 1981 by Manna Music, Inc., used by permission; from "Great is Thy Faithfulness" by Thomas O. Chisholm, copyright © 1923, renewed 1951 by Hope Publishing Co., Carol Stream, IL 60188, all rights reserved, used by permission; from "Hope of the World" by Georgia Harkness, copyright © 1954, renewed 1982 by The Hymn Society, Texas Christian University, Fort Worth, TX 76129, all rights reserved, used by permission.

For information address:

Hope Publishing House
P. O. Box 60008
Pasadena, California 91116 - U.S.A.

Cover design - Greg Endries Design

Cover picture - Suzanne Atkinson

Printed in the U.S.A. on acid-free paper.

Library of Congress Cataloging-in-Publication Data

Goard, Dottie Mae, 1925.
  These last days : angelic messengers reveal the future / Dottie Mae Goard
    p.   cm.
  ISBN 0-932727-73-5 (pbk.) : $11.95
  1. Goard, Dottie Mae--Diaries. 2. Christian biography--United States.
3. Visions. 4. Private revelations. 5. Prophecies. 6. Second Advent.
  I. Title
  BR1725.S246A3   1994
  248.2'9--dc20   94-10219
                                                          CIP

This book is dedicated:

To the glory of God, the love of Jesus Christ and the fellowship of the Holy Spirit;

To the memory of my husband Howard Goard who faithfully supported me through the writing of this book and the struggle of learning to operate a computer, who was always ready to jump into the next adventure and who sat in church praying by my side for many years;

To my sister Betty and my brother Basil who helped me to grow up.

Acknowledgements

My deep appreciation goes to my very dear friend Della Craighead who has advised, supported and encouraged me throughout the writing of this book; to Karin Hartline, Joyce Bond and Cleonne Smith for their painstaking review of content and grammar; and to Suzanne Atkinson who painted the face of Jesus for the cover.

A special word of thanks goes to Faith Annette Sand, my editor and publisher, for her skill in preparing the book for publication and for her kindness, her prayers and the tender loving care with which she has dealt with me.

Last and greatest of all, I offer thanks to my Lord and Savior Jesus Christ who has led me by the hand throughout the living of these experiences and who has guided and supported me in the sharing of them with the world.

Preface

"Publish glad tidings" was the word that came to me from the Lord last week. Seven years of journaling have provided insights into God's divine nature that may be helpful to someone else. "Show others how one may grow in knowledge of me and my love," the Lord said.

It started with a grief. A dear friend of many years moved to Houston where our friendship continued in phone calls, letters and an occasional visit. One day Beth called from a hospital saying she had brain cancer. In three weeks she was dead—and I had been allowed no last visit to say good-bye or become adjusted to the finality of earthly relationships.

Soon after this my friend Miriam took me to the home of her friend Hazel who has the gift of prophecy. After a time of prayer, Hazel told me Beth is in heaven ringing joy bells—and I would be receiving a message from her by way of the Lord—the only one who can bridge the chasm between earth and heaven. Little did I know what tremendous impact and change those messages, not only one but two, would have on my life.

I left Hazel's home dejected because she had said there *was a message*, but where was it? I looked down at the small tape recorder I had taken with me. Perhaps if I listened again to the conversation, something would be revealed. Back home, I sat down and turned on the tape. There, to my wondering ears, in the midst of the conversation about "joy bells of heaven," were the high sweet tinkling chimes of *bells ringing!* The Lord was actually allowing me to hear the ringing of the joy bells of heaven. I wept as I listened again and again to that recording of those bells. What a great and magnificent message they brought me: 1. Heaven is real; 2. God is real and near; and 3. God cares about us. Later, I was to learn firsthand some other certainties about God, but for then it was sufficient to know these three.

The second message to come from Beth through the Lord occurred a few weeks later while I was gathering material to take camping. I reached for a book Beth had given me by Richard Shelton, *Selected Poems, 1969 - 1981,* and it fell open to a poem called "Valediction." The theme of the poem is a message from someone who has died and left behind certain things.

> ... I am resigning from my shoes
> they are worn out
> and will fit anybody
>
> whoever wears them
> his job will be to harvest
> the wrinkled shells of walnuts ...

I stored this poem in my memory and did not recall it until several days later when I was tired, knees hurting, unable to think clearly. Could it be that I was beginning to sail over the edge of sanity and all these God experiences were only my vivid imagination? I mentioned Beth in my prayers. Stumbling over a throw rug, I looked down, and there at my feet on the rug was *a fragment of a wrinkled shell of a walnut!*

Shortly after this I began writing a daily journal of my pilgrimage. The most important entries are contained in the body of this book. All names, excepting my own and those of my family, have been changed.

In the beginning, I had no idea where my writing was going. I was content merely to chronicle my learning to know God in slow, sometimes painful, steps. This seemed a worthy enough project. However, as time progressed, new revelations were given and the real purpose of the book began to surface. Beginning in the 1989 Christmas season, God revealed the first of three startling prophecies which were to be delivered to those from every nation who have ears to hear. The last prophecy came in February 1991. It now seems that the delivery of these messages is the real purpose of the book. They can only be understood within the context of the entire book.

—*Dottie Mae Goard*
Bartlesville, Oklahoma

February 27, 1984—

Today my sister celebrates another birthday. Betty is a little older than I and is permitted to try on each new year before I come to it. This can be either a help or a hindrance, depending on the circumstances.

In matters of experiencing new school classes or riding a bicycle or getting married, it can be enormously helpful. But because she hated piano lessons and cried before and after every one, I chose not to partake and have been sorry ever since. She stood up for me whenever I was in trouble, read the comics aloud before I was literate, drove us out to Uncle Amos' swimming pool on Sunday afternoons when she was 16 and I was 14, and allowed me to tag around with her gang through most of our growing up.

But today she is deeply depressed in spirit and is even questioning the existence of God. After telephoning and comforting her, I began to explore the enduring implications of friendship and love. It dawned on me that I would volunteer to go to hell with my sister, if she were there, to keep her company.

Instead Jesus came to earth and took the hell of the cross to be with us in all our hells, self-inflicted and otherwise. Christ came to keep the company of everyone, friend and enemy. Would I volunteer to go to hell for my enemies? But if love were taken into hell, would it still be hell? Conversely, if our loved ones are not in heaven with us, would it still be heaven?

March 10, 1984 —

I walked the winter prairie alone this morning. A great expanse of light-brown grasses stretched ahead as far as I could see, interrupted only by the cross-hatching of section-line fences. The prairie appeared as dead as the reddish-brown leaves of bluestem grasses curled upward around central seed-bearing stalks that long since had scattered their crop. Between these dried clumps appeared the green of wild grasses already up. The quickening of the grasses animated my spirit, somehow assuaging the anxiety over my sister's emotional state.

Stooping, I saw nestled among the green sprouts tiny bluets, one of the first flowers to bloom after the snow melts. This flower, only half as wide as my fingernail, is as carefully and lovingly made by the One who also made me. Nearby peeked out another early flower—the spring beauty—admired by all for its delicate lines of red and purple through a creamy petal.

While concentrating on these small flowers, I became aware of a distant moan, not unlike the sound of a small boy blowing across a bottle. On the far knoll, over a mile away, prairie chickens were courting. Sound traveled far in that spring stillness and though I couldn't see them even with binoculars, I knew the cocks were performing their intricate, luring dance.

Continuing to scan with binoculars, I noticed a coyote trotting leisurely across a high ridge. The tail-down posture made the animal appear dejected, but this natural carriage only serves to hide the hunter from vulnerable prey.

Tramping on, I came to a hill overlooking the wide river valley. The sun was well up and the meadowlarks, perched on some persimmon sprouts, were singing from their hearts. Easing myself down on an exposed rock, I listened to them while watching a marsh hawk patrol the valley below. Perhaps I could invite my sister here. A day on this prairie would do much to lift her spirits and I could talk to her about the Lord.

March 17, 1984—

I do love this earth and appreciate the stewardship over it God has given us. Sometimes, when my hands become very warm with the Spirit, I would like to take these healing hands and wrap them around the whole earth, comforting the cut trees and broken bushes, healing the scarred land and flooded valleys, recovering the displaced wildlife, as well as the abused creatures, people and places on earth. I want to drape peace over the land, heal people and console them, sweeping my warm hands through the poisoned air to cleanse and purify it.

Why does not God do this outright? Alas, we were made free beings—free to do good or evil and free to live with the consequences of either or both.

April 25, 1984—

The "Peter and Paul" movie was on television tonight. God, would I risk myself to a most horrible death as those two did to perpetuate the gospel?

April 28, 1984—

Tonight, my husband Howard and I ate at a restaurant next to a family with a little girl who looked ill. She had dark circles under her eyes and I wondered whether she was suffering from leukemia or something equally serious. I began to pray for her, asking that peace and healing cover her. I know she felt the power of God through the prayer because she turned in her chair and looked at me a long time. I wanted to reach out and touch her, but there was no opportunity.

May 9, 1984—

All last weekend I spent bird-watching for warblers, neglecting Bible reading, rest, soul-searching and intense prayer. When I did pray, it seemed empty. I learned a lesson on what to prioritize in life: If God is not put first, God is not there.

It is true that the Holy Spirit can reach us more easily when we have not eaten, or have eaten lightly. I have to fight constantly against eating too much.

May 10, 1984—

Could it be the black man in the library to whom I gave lunch money today was sent by Christ, or was Christ personified? He was wet, cold and ragged and I couldn't bear to think of his being hungry too so I gave him all I had—five dollars. He cried when I handed it to him but he needed more help than I could give.

Twice I have awakened in the night to a voice calling my name. It was a male voice, a tenor.

May 18, 1984—

The kingdom of God is real. Jesus meant it when he said the kingdom is upon us. Life can have moments of stunning beauty. This morning after prayer I walked to the woods by the river and stood silently, watching the sky and green leaves, praising God for such loveliness and peace. It was as though the birds sensed the kingdom in the moment, for as I stood there, more and more birds gathered in the trees and bushes around me. Some sang, others only flitted around a little until I saw them, and then they perched quietly on an exposed twig.

Two men with rifles walked along the path toward me. I was not afraid, feeling that they would not harm me. We spoke, and I ambled back to my car.

May 23, 1984—

Christians and Jews are talking about the same goals but using different terms. When the Jews talk about the Messiah and the messianic kingdom, they expect peace to abound—the lion and the lamb lying down together and a child playing over the snake pit with no danger. They are talking about the same thing Christians do when we speak of the kingdom of God.

When I experienced the kingdom encircling me down at the river with its beauty, peace and wildlife, that was only a segment of the kingdom. The Jews, however, expect the messianic age to be enforced by a Messiah, established by law, and compulsory for everyone. Christians realize it is voluntary—from the heart—and that it can be experienced individually.

May 29, 1984—

The Palmers' grandchild, Alice, fell from a swing and is in terrible pain. The diagnosis is spinal cancer. Today I entreated God to heal her with his resurrection power and even offered to give the child the rest of my life if she needed it.

May 30, 1984—

I am asking God for the gift of tongues. I sit quietly and pray aloud, thinking, if he sends it, I will be ready.

May 31, 1984—

The doctor says a black spot on my face may be cancerous and should be cut out. I am inclined to wait until Miriam and Hazel come back to pray for me. Meanwhile, last Friday my Emmaus group laid hands on me and prayed for healing. I was not worried; in fact, I felt tremendously warmed throughout.

Robert Bowerman invited my husband and me to be part of the evangelism committee. I hesitated answering, desiring freedom to do my own projects, but the Lord called me to accountability by reminding me of the wrinkled shells of walnuts which are waiting to be harvested. I told Robert we would.

June 6, 1984—

The Bible opened today to Zechariah 13:9, *And I will put this third into the fire, refine them as one refines silver, and test them as gold is tested.* Perhaps God is refining and testing me by this facial spot. These experiences I am having are so powerful and so real, nothing else seems important.

June 11, 1984—

I asked God again about the black spot on my face and found my answer opening the Bible to the story Luke tells of the neighbor who goes to borrow bread at night and wins by being persistent. Then comes the famous, *"Ask, and it will be given you; search, and you will find; knock, and the door will be opened to you. For everyone who asks receives ... "* (11:9-10).

Praise God! I will be healed! My friend is pestering me to go to the doctor. She says Billy Graham and Oral Roberts go to doctors and have operations. Is she the voice of reason or is she doing the work of Satan, trying to cause me to doubt God?

June 13, 1984—

Last Thursday night I attended an ordination service for deacons and elders in the Methodist church. During the long drive home, my hands and body became very warm with the Spirit. It's true one feels the Spirit more when other believers are present, as Matthew says, *"For where two or three are gathered in my name, I am there among them"* (18:20).

June 20, 1984—

The child Alice is better! Praise the Lord! She is going home from the hospital today to recuperate from the radiation and chemotherapy. Lord, bless her and continue to heal her.

July 3, 1984—

Lord, please send me courage to live by the Spirit and not by the world's rules. It has been a year since Beth died. I think of her often and how much we will have to talk about. Perhaps she could send a hint about how to receive the gift of tongues. It would enable me to use God's power of healing better, though a smattering has already come.

July 7, 1984—

We were driving across the vast flat wheatland of Kansas. As I took a turn driving, I prayed with eyes open, thanking God for the beauty of this land, realizing that the hand that created it created us, and the Spirit that sustains it sustains us. How can heaven be more beautiful than this life? It is like living in a new and different dimension. According to John Sherrill in *They Speak With Other Tongues,* the Holy Spirit dwells within people whose thoughts and actions are pure, who welcome the Lord, converse with God, trust in God and love God. Also, the Spirit remains only if we give away the love we receive.

July 8, 1984—

Miriam heard about a man who travels around Europe helping people, touching and blessing them. Perhaps on this trip I can warm some cold hearts and put joy in some weary lives.

July 10, 1984—

The opportunity presented itself immediately to cheer and comfort people. In every location we have stopped, I have sought out someone to talk with. Last night we invited a single elderly man who was tent camping to eat dinner with us and tell us about himself. He was from Florida and was spending six weeks driving around the country. I opened the subject of God and church, and he said he had been seeking God for a long time. We told him how important God is in our lives. The next morning, when I went to say good-bye to him, I looked directly into his eyes and told him to continue searching for God for God is real and near, and the search is worthwhile. He knew how serious I was, and he nodded.

We have traveled through the most beautiful country on earth. There have been high snow-crowned mountains and deep-green pine forests, barley fields on top of rolling plateaus as far as the eye could see, clear mountain run-off streams, and lakes so blue they appear black. Throughout the trip, I have sung hymns and praised God.

When I have a need, a song will come to mind with words that give the greatest amount of help and comfort. This morning it was, "O, rest in the Lord; wait patiently on him." I must not forget devotions, Bible reading and prayer.

July 24, 1984—

I have been with my dear friend Meg at a convention for several days but until yesterday have had no time alone with her. For a week, God has been putting into my mind the hymn, "I Love to Tell the Story." With trembling knees, but a determined heart, I told her about the joy bells of heaven, about God speaking to me in various ways and my hearing and doing what God says. I told her of the healing power the Lord has sent, and that power is given to one who loves people and God, has faith in God, and is obedient to his will. I told her some of my experiences and how God revealed it was he who was contacting me. She listened attentively but said very little.

As soon as I told Meg these things, the Lord sent a gift of the Spirit: "patience." The Scripture calls it a fruit of the Spirit, but it surely seemed like a gift and came from beyond me. I became so patient with things that normally would have irritated me. Patience, then, may be more valuable than the gift of tongues. Galatians tells us after conversion Paul withdrew for three years to pray and study. I must remember God's wisdom doesn't immediately drop on a convert; it takes time, patience, prayer, meditation, study, sacrifice and love. God is so patient.

God just pointed out to me that it also takes testing. The Bible fell open to James: *My brothers and sisters, whenever you face trials of any kind, consider it nothing but joy, because you know that the testing of your faith produces endurance; and let endurance have its full effect, so that you may be mature and complete, lacking in nothing. If any of you is lacking in wisdom, ask God, who gives to all generously and ungrudgingly, and it will be given you. But ask in faith, never doubting, for the one who doubts is like a wave of the sea, driven and tossed by the wind* (1:2-6).

Also today the Lord opened the Bible to 2 Corinthians: *And all of us, with unveiled faces, seeing the glory of the Lord as though reflected in a mirror, are being transformed into the same image from one degree of glory to another, for this comes from the Lord, the Spirit* (3:18). Perhaps this explains why my body seems to be in the process of healing and rejuvenating in many ways.

July 28, 1984—

On the way home, we stopped in Denver to see our old friends Irene and Joe. Joe has been very ill for a long time and Irene looked as if she had aged a great deal. She welcomed us with open arms and tears. I do not know God's will for him, but I have been praying for him for many months. Just perhaps he will live. I prayed for Irene to receive peace and for God to make himself known to her and to comfort her.

August 13, 1984—

Home life is wonderful. The prayers of our friends and the anointing with oil is helping. The evil force that has been plaguing us has been driven out. I called Irene and she said Joe is better—has a higher blood count, is eating, has more energy and feels better. Praise God! Perhaps he will be allowed to regain his health. Howard said the new medicine must be helping, but I said medicine doesn't create new blood cells. He nodded.

August 14, 1984—

Miriam's friend Pat saw my black facial spot in a vision last night and told me to go to a doctor. While Miriam and I were pondering this at lunch, she received a message from God that I should be willing to seek help from others for my problem, else I might rise on a pedestal Satan could pull down. In other words try a little *humility*. *That* did it. I canceled my trip to Missouri and will see a doctor tomorrow. Miriam also reported Jesus saying, "I have almost shown you my face!" Whew! What an astonishing message!

August 15, 1984 —

I learned a valuable lesson in humility. I must not expect God to do my bidding but must pray to do his. God's will, not mine, be done. My facial blemish is a cancerous growth. It can and will be removed immediately and I may be all right. In any case, I am all right. *Whether in life or in death, I am the Lord's.*

August 16, 1984, 2:30 A.M. —

The awesome, God-filled life I am learning to live is so much more important than a puny illness. This cancer is, in a sense, my prison—like Paul's—which should only serve to strengthen me in the faith. Dad [Howard's father] finally showed some concern for me today. He cried when I told him my problem.

Jesus was with me yesterday throughout the whole day's events. He rode with me to the city, sat with me in the doctor's office, surrounded me with peace and love, and even pointed out butterflies flying by the seventh story window.

August 23, 1984 —

Praise God! The tumor was *non-malignant!* The doctors were very surprised. The Lord has been with me all along, protecting me from that devil, malignancy. I felt no pain, either at the time of surgery or later when the anesthetic wore off. Now, I am free to press on with my life and work. A new neighbor moved in. I asked if they have a church. They do.

September 1, 1984 —

Last week I witnessed to everyone I saw—old friends from several congregations, my beauty operator, people in nursing homes, et al. Some only looked at me strangely.

September 7, 1984 —

Yesterday I was working with the string trimmer and ran it into my tennis shoe. It hurt so badly I yelled, hopping toward the porch to see what damage was done. Then I remembered Charlie, our young minister, told us to praise the Lord for everything, even bad things. I yelled, "Praise the Lord" several times and the pain stopped within three seconds. I examined my foot and there was no mark, no bruise and no soreness later. When I told Howard about it, he listened but didn't answer.

According to Psalms 22:3, God resides in the praises of people. I have started praying intently for Ruth Ballentine, whose digestive system was so badly damaged by chemotherapy, always asking for God's will in the matter. Strangely, my stomach has been out of order since praying for her. Sometimes, I have sympathy pains with the person I care about.

September 15, 1984 —

Joe died. His last weeks were comfortable, then he just died. Irene is devastated. I will see her next week in Springfield at the grave-side services.

September 25, 1984 —

Young Alice has cancer cells in the spinal fluid again. I must ask my Emmaus group to pray. Confirmation came this morning that she will get well. I opened the Bible "by chance" to John 4:47-54, ... *Jesus said to him, "Go; your son will live." The man believed the word that Jesus spoke* ... Praise God! The only question in mind is whether her parents need to believe she will be healed for her to recover. Both Miriam and I have asked the Lord to post angels around her.

Yesterday I visited two old friends. During the conversation,

I spoke of my new religious experiences and my feeling that God is with me and that Beth is in heaven ringing joy bells. They looked at me strangely and changed the subject.

A week ago we invited Mr. Parker, the old man who lives down the street, to dinner. God directed me to serve fried chicken and mashed potatoes. I already had the chicken, but only one small potato. God said to look in the refrigerator. *There,* where I never put potatoes, was the largest potato I have ever seen, plenty big enough to make mashed potatoes for three—and it made the best mashed potatoes we ever ate. Mr. Parker ate two big helpings. Afterward, while cleaning up, I said to God, "Too bad you were not able to enjoy those delicious mashed potatoes with us."

He shot back, "Who do you think made them?"

October 16, 1984—

Alice's grandmother indicated that both grandparents and parents have given up on Alice. I'm sorry they have, but I have not. I understood a long time ago that she would be healed, and everything I get from the Lord affirms that. I opened the Bible by chance to Matthew 24:13, *"But the one who endures to the end will be saved."* Then later I came upon James, *Be patient, therefore, beloved, until the coming of the Lord. The farmer waits for the precious crop from the earth, being patient with it until it receives the early and the late rains. You also must be patient. Strengthen your hearts, for the coming of the Lord is near ... As an example of suffering and patience, beloved, take the prophets who spoke in the name of the Lord. ... And you have seen the purpose of the Lord, how the Lord is compassionate and merciful. ... Are any among you sick? They should call for the elders of the church and have them pray over them, anointing them with oil in the name of the Lord. The prayer of faith will save the sick, and the Lord will raise them up; and anyone who has committed sins will be forgiven. ... The prayer of the righteous is powerful and effective* (5:7-8, 10-11, 14-16).

This latter verse emphasizes the need of the one who wants to call down healing from the Lord to be righteous. Sigh! I am trying, but frequently fail. Forgive me Lord.

This brings the question of why the prayers of some are answered with a *No*. If the Spirit is not dwelling in you because the Lord is uncomfortable with your life and thoughts, then your prayers are too faint to be heard above your life-style. Since God and the Lord's gifts are subject to humans, if these restraints were not in place, God's wondrous miracles would be on call to serve unrighteous people. But, even then, God is merciful and eager to help if we turn to the Lord with our lives. We must note that this is the message of the prophets.

The reason the prophets of the Old Testament and John the Baptist kept preaching repentance is that unless we turn back from unrighteousness and make our lives fertile for the indwelling Spirit to take root, the kingdom of God cannot progress on this earth.

October 21, 1984—

Today while working, I started singing, "O divine redeemer, I pray thee grant me pardon and remember not, O Lord, my sins." This hymn kept coming back to me repeatedly. Then I remembered telling Mr. Bailey this morning that I would not be able to teach a literacy student, heard his disappointed voice, and felt guilty all morning and well into the afternoon.

Taking time to sit down and think, I remembered the apostle Paul and how he said no one could perfectly fulfil the

Law and that's what grace and forgiveness are for. So the song was a reminder that though I am not perfect, I am forgiven! Thank you, Jesus.

October 27, 1984 —

Yesterday, I had lunch with Alice's grandmother. I told her of my certainty that Alice is going to get well. She said she hoped so, for that is the only chance she has since the doctors have given up on her. She also told me people around the world are praying for her. Maybe this will give her hope.

Last night, about 12:30 A.M., I awakened, noticing my chest was warm with deep Spirit heat similar to what I received when people were praying for me at the time of the facial surgery. The Spirit heat slowly drifted down into my abdomen, then my legs, one at a time, then my feet, one at a time. After it subsided, I put on a robe and slippers and sat in the living room praying.

November 1, 1984 —

Alice is better! She is not needing additional blood transfusions and is livelier than she has been for months! Praise God!

November 8, 1984 —

Last night we held the prayer for healing service for Alice in the chapel. This in itself was a miracle because the chapel had been designated for another meeting. There were nearly 30 people present, many of whom I did not call. We sang and read Scripture and we each prayed as the Spirit inspired us. Everyone was moved and many tears were wiped away. Miriam saw a brilliant white light engulfing the chapel as we prayed. The Lord is indeed quick to save.

Many of the fresh flowers sent to me three weeks ago were still good. I added some petunias from our garden that had persisted in spite of freezes—another miracle—and took them to the service. By this God demonstrated that the Lord could save fresh flowers from freezing and cut flowers without root; therefore, God could surely save a small girl in the midst of spinal cancer. Praise God! My hands are hot as I write this.

Miriam's vision of negativity around Alice, and how it needed to be corrected in order to finish the healing, was the reason for this service. It was to convince Alice's family to believe in her healing by the love of Christ.

November 9, 1984—

Yesterday I felt so wonderful and joyful all day. The sky was prettier than I had ever seen it. The color of the sky is symbolic of the purity and perfectness of God's love. It looks so clean and fresh. The clouds scurrying across it exemplify the many moods of his Divine personality. Today, it is laughter.

November 13, 1984—

They took Alice back to the hospital for more chemotherapy, and now she is critical because of heart failure, pneumonia and brain damage from the heart problem. At first, I was upset because I felt that God had let us down, that God had promised the child would live. Then, I shored up my faith, (and Miriam's, bless her), and we confirmed God is faithful and can do all things. God can even bring back the dead, so surely God can heal one small child.

Miriam and I are the only ones who still believe she will be restored. The Lord is always faithful to his promises, though his timing is according to his own will.

November 15, 1984 —

I heard this morning that Alice is on a respirator. in a deep, irreversible coma with extensive brain damage. I am giving her to God. God's will, not mine, be done. I have reached the "but if not" stage.

When Shadrack, Meshach and Abednego came before King Nebuchadnezzar, they said, *"O Nebuchadnezzar, we have no need to present a defense to you in this matter. If our God whom we serve is able to deliver us from the furnace of blazing fire and out of your hand, O king, let him deliver us. But if not, be it known to you, O king, that we will not serve your gods and we will not worship the golden statue that you have set up"* (Dan 3:16-18).

I know God can do all things and if it is the Lord's divine will, he can raise up Alice, restore every cell in her brain and heart and kidneys and hand her to her parents. "But if not," I will still worship and praise the Lord.

November 21, 1984 —

Jesus trusted God and was crucified. His healing came at the Resurrection. Perhaps that is when Alice's will be healed.

I feel as though I have striven with God as did Jacob of old.

This afternoon, I wakened from a nap singing, "My faith is based on nothing less than Jesus' love and righteousness. Upon the solid rock I stand; All other ground is sinking sand; all other ground is sinking sand."

Early last week, Miriam saw a vision of Alice surrounded by a beautiful white light and felt a complete and powerful wave of peace concerning her. I had a dream of Jesus waiting in a garden for her and I also felt complete peace.

I do indeed believe that love is the only thing that lasts after death. Nothing else endures, no matter what good works are done; only the love that initiated and resulted from the good works. I will strive to love more. If love is really the only thing of importance, we surely do spend a lot of time and money on worthless pursuits.

November 25, 1984 —

I was walking alone by the lake today. My hands had not become hot while praying and I wondered where I had slipped. Looking at the sky, with feathery streaks of clouds decorating it, I noticed gulls flying over, some flapping lightly, some soaring. I felt warmed by such beauty and purity. A message came then that God does not ask for my dying in exchange for Alice's life, but God does ask for my *life*—my living a total life given to his will and purposes. And the Lord assured me that he will take care of Alice in his own way. Amen.

November 29, 1984 —

I am becoming ever more convinced there are two ways the world operates. One is natural—producing neutral, scientific and material action and interaction. This is the way 90 to 98 percent of the world operates. The other lives by an entirely different standard—the kingdom of God, defined as love-centered, love-controlled action which may be well beyond the scientific ways normally expected. It can consist of impossible healings, control of all events including storms and earthquakes, mental knowledge and foreknowledge of prophets, wisdom beyond belief and absolute spiritual control of material things.

The kingdom standard becomes possible to those who put love first, humble themselves to live under the control of God, and trust God completely and implicitly. The three words are love, trust and obedience.

December 1, 1984—

Alice is dead. Yesterday I was stunned, numb, unable to think or pray effectively. I didn't feel anything.

This morning the Bible opened by chance to Ephesians 6:10-18: *Finally, be strong in the Lord and in the strength of his power. Put on the whole armor of God, so that you may be able to stand against the wiles of the devil. For our struggle is not against enemies of blood and flesh, but against the rulers, against authorities, against the cosmic powers of this present darkness, against the spiritual forces of evil in the heavenly places. Therefore take up the whole armor of God, so that you may be able to withstand on that evil day, and having done everything, to stand firm. Stand therefore, and fasten the belt of truth around your waist, and put on the breastplate of righteousness. As shoes for your feet put on whatever will make you ready to proclaim the gospel of peace. With all of these, take the shield of faith, with which you will be able to quench all the flaming arrows of the evil one. Take the helmet of salvation, and the sword of the Spirit, which is the word of God.* Thank you, Lord. Then God reminded me that Jesus thought he had failed when he was on the cross, and even said, *My God, why have you forsaken me.*

January 3, 1985—

It has been a while since I had the inspiration to write in this journal. There is a great deal to say about the peace that comes after January 1.

I asked the Lord what I should do and the Scriptures opened by chance to Acts 11:1-20—the story of Peter's vision of all animals on earth being clean and Peter being sent to Caesarea to preach to Gentiles. This must mean that God will direct my course as he did Peter's.

January 7, 1985 —

Yesterday at dusk, we watched the full moon rise over Copan Lake where we had gone to identify ducks. This morning the full moon was setting in the west and I thought, "The Lord saw to getting the moon across the sky while I slept. I did not have to worry about it or watch it or will it. The Lord took care of it. The Lord is in charge of this universe and of my life. All I have to do is trust. Thank you, Father."

January 11, 1985 —

At Emmaus tonight I witnessed to a man who was troubled over the meaning of the kingdom of God. I told him it was glorious and loving and healing and not of the natural "law of gravity" world. Later the Bible opened to Psalms 145:10-13: *All your works shall give thanks to you, O Lord, and all your faithful shall bless you. They shall speak of the glory of your kingdom, and tell of your power, to make known to all people your mighty deeds, and the glorious splendor of your kingdom. Your kingdom is an everlasting kingdom, and your dominion endures throughout all generations.* Praise the Lord! He is here and listening and comforting and supporting us continually!

January 17, 1985 —

I have anointed my feet, face, neck and body with holy oil, also the house including doors and windows. In the Old Testament the Israelites tacked the Law of God to their doors, also wore it on their foreheads, arms and loins. This accomplished the same results as anointing, bringing God's healing and loving blessings to the house and their bodies. Think of the blessings enjoyed by the woman who washed Jesus' feet with her tears and dried them with her hair, and the one who anointed his head with oil!

January 31, 1985 –

The Lord instructed me to write to Rose, an acquaintance from long ago, who is ill with bone cancer and tell her about him, for she has always been a non-believer. This is a difficult task because Rose and I have been at cross-purposes for many years. So I sent this as part of a letter to her last week:

1. The world was created by one great unified power we call God. Creatures were placed on it for the purpose of enjoying life and learning to love each other and God.

2. We are likely to be stuck throughout all eternity with the ability to love which we learn while here.

3. There is a spiritual realm to reality that we shall be living in when the physical realm ceases. This spiritual realm is without physical dimensions, including time.

4. The spiritual realm is available to all who want it. You have to ask.

5. The power, God, that created all that is, cares about this creation and deals kindly with both physical and spiritual reality. God knows all things including thoughts, motives and intentions.

6. God desires only good for all creation.

7. God desires for all creatures: love, trust and obedience to his will – righteousness.

8. In response to this love, trust and obedience, God's creatures are given profound joy and peace, hope for a spiritual existence beyond death, wholeness or healing of body and spirit in this physical life – and absolute fearlessness. Salvation and healing mean the same thing. If God be for us, no one or nothing can be against us – neither death nor pain nor loneliness nor fear nor anything. People have gone singing to their deaths because they knew it was only a passing stage to the next encounter and they knew they were loved and cared for by the one who created them and all that is.

9. How do we know all this? Someone came from beyond the physical to tell us. Then that person was killed because imperfect people couldn't stand a perfect person

in their midst. He forgave them as they were killing him and after being dead three days, he rose to life again and lived 40 more days before disappearing. During these 40 days, hundreds saw him.

10. I know this more than I know my own name because he has spoken to me—to my heart. He directs my life and I am living in absolute joy and in the most wonderful peace anyone can imagine. I am completely and utterly unafraid. My mental and emotional health are great and my physical health is better than in many years.

11. The person from the beyond, who is Jesus, has sent me to tell you to have faith in God and know that he not only loves and cares for you, but wants you to trust him with your life—not to be afraid or angry—and know you are in his loving hands in life or in death.

12. You have only to embrace and accept this message.

February 7, 1985 —

We are in Tallahassee, Florida, on our way further south. I am driving our little Toyota behind Howard in the mini-motor home. The Lord has been with us throughout the entire journey. We could not have made it through the snow and ice during the first two days without divine help. Once I nearly despaired of steering through a six-inch mixture of snow and ice which the Toyota was high-centering. Rounding a corner, I saw standing up starkly against the sky, the clean lines of a church steeple and cross. I knew then we would be safe. The message from *God Calling,* edited by A.J. Russell, for the day we started, said to go step-by-step and God would help us. Once when I noticed Howard was not ahead, I glanced up and saw a brilliant blue sky looking especially beautiful and knew we were safe. God has a way of telling us not to worry but to trust. We have prayed daily for the Lord's protection along the way.

March 1, 1985 –

There is peace in this camper—and beauty right outside its door. God makes everything so perfect that every place we look displays a picture more beautiful than any person can paint or photograph. When I am tuned in to God's Spirit, the vividness of every scene is beyond description. When everything is ordinary, I wonder where I went astray. This morning I sat alone on a picnic bench near the canal and watched, prayed and listened for a long time. How would it be to look up in that beautiful sky and see the face of Jesus? At once a hymn surfaced, and I started singing, "I Would See Jesus."

An ancient truth of Roman Catholic tradition has impressed me: Jesus *is present* in Holy Communion. I believe that if Jesus is so present in oil—which has been blessed—so a change can be noted in what has been anointed, then Jesus can be and is present in the Eucharist. It is not just "in memory," but a real presence. This came to me last Sunday as we were taking Communion at a Methodist church in Ft. Myers.

If this be so, one really should partake often, perhaps daily, or certainly weekly. It should make a striking difference in physical, mental and spiritual health. Also, this presence must be what Paul the Apostle meant when he said, *For all who eat and drink without discerning the body, eat and drink judgment against themselves* (1 Cor 11:29).

Howard and I even noticed an actual difference in the taste of a bottle of grape juice we took to church to be blessed and used for Communion. We brought the remainder along with us on this trip. As we were drinking it, we both commented that it tasted so good, extraordinarily so. When we bought the same brand a few days later, it tasted like ordinary grape juice.

March 2, 1985 –

As an extension of yesterday's statements about Communion bringing blessings and healing to people who partake with the right attitude, I had an additional revelation. In like manner, saying a blessing over food at mealtime, in a sense, does the same thing. We aren't just thanking God for furnishing the food and pleasure of eating, we are asking God's blessing on it so that eating it will be like anointing with holy oil or taking Communion, and bring healing and wholeness to the recipient.

March 12, 1985 –

We arrived home safely Sunday night. God was with us the entire trip. Traveling back, when I needed assurance, God spoke through the brilliant blue of the sky. On the last day it was cloudy all day. From time to time in the afternoon I wondered how God could send comfort with the sky overcast. Immediately, the sun came out and shone briefly on the highway and car.

One of the last miracles of the trip occurred when I stepped on a fire ant hill while walking on a dike at St. Mark's Wildlife Refuge in Florida. We had stopped to look at a sora rail skulking in and out of the reeds beside the dike. I stepped on something soft, but didn't move or look down for fear of spooking the sora. When I finally looked down, I saw my pants covered with fire ants. Crying out, I jumped back into Howard's arms. I took both hands and swept them off, pulling up my pant legs and raking ants from my bare legs. Howard held me up as I pulled off my sneakers and whisked ants from my socks and out of my shoes with bare hands. When I had finished, Howard ventured, "Dottie, those are fire ants! Didn't they sting?"

I said, "No, Praise God!" O God, how great thou art!

March 28, 1985 –

This morning I went to Langston's Field to look for early warblers. It was cloudy, windy and cold as I started toward the clearing where an old jeep road ambles down to the river. There I stopped and waited. Soon the clouds lifted showing a fragment of sky painted the most beautiful blue I've ever seen which reminded me of a book about a woman who died, went to heaven and returned to report seeing an exquisitely gorgeous blue sky and vivid green grass.

This started me thinking about heaven and I hoped for clouds in heaven too, because they adorn the sky in new raiment constantly. Then I thought about heavenly trees and flowers and singing birds.

At that instant, the trees down the river began to take on magnificent intensity of color. Tiny new leaves flashed a flaming gold. The shades of green were myriad and unworldly. Everything looked as though a divine spotlight were behind it to magnify and glorify the color. Never have I seen such beauty before. Thank you, Lord, for your wonderful gift. Indeed, a very thin veil separates earth from heaven.

April 5, 1985 –

I was angry the other night, and it was justified. But when I went to my prayer closet, the Spirit was not there. I said, "Where are you, Lord? I can't find you anyplace." The next morning, I knew it was not the Lord who had moved. I had gone away from the Constant One. I asked forgiveness and the Spirit returned. The Lord is teaching me so much. How can I possibly thank God enough. O, the wonder of having the Holy Lord God—who created everything that is—stoop to speak to me and teach me and love me. How wondrous is this place!

The Lord keeps reminding me of the importance of witnessing—spreading the word of the salvation of Christ. This is more important than any other religious duty.

April 8, 1985 —

Last Saturday morning in preparation for Easter, our Monday prayer team walked around the church at six, praying, singing, reciting Psalms and anointing doors and windows with holy oil.

Afterward we went inside where it was quite dark. I walked up to anoint the pulpit with oil and said a prayer aloud asking the Lord to fill the sanctuary so all who entered would feel the presence of the Resurrected Christ and be filled with God's love, peace and joy. Just then the sanctuary started *lighting up!* A pinkish glow began permeating everything in fine detail over the entire sanctuary. The room became lighter and lighter, and there were *no shadows* in normally dark corners, not even the balcony.

I was in such awe, I had to grasp the railing to keep from falling. When the prayer ended, I turned to go down the steps. Everything went black and I almost fell down the steps. As I had prayed for the Holy Spirit to enter the sanctuary, *this had happened,* and that was the light! How can it be that this powerful ruler of the universe is visiting us and answering us and responding to our prayers?

April 13, 1985 —

I have been thinking about peace on a national level. God has shown through intervention in my personal life that *I know* I am protected from calamity with divine intervention. God *told* the Israelites throughout their history the Lord would protect them "as a hen would gather her chicks under her wing," if they would turn from their evil ways and seek the Lord.

Likewise, I believe God will truly protect this nation, or any country, if the people as a whole will turn from evil, seek righteousness, and claim the forgiveness of Christ. If our country—as a people—would seek forgiveness for past sins and commit their lives to righteousness, God will protect this nation from all evil.

April 19, 1985 –

I mowed the lawn this hot, humid morning. A paper shell white narcissus bloom appeared in a corner of the yard where one has never been before. I knew the Lord was comforting me with that surprise. The mower sputtered a little at one point, indicating it was out of gas. However, it revived to mow another ten minutes until the lawn was finished. Then the mower died just as I bent over to turn it off, having run the last ten minutes on gasoline supplied by the Lord. Sheer perfection is the way the Lord operates!

April 29, 1985 –

I felt a great desire to go to the chapel to pray this afternoon. At one point, I moved from the altar to a nearby pew and started reading a pew Bible by the light coming through stained glass windows. Again, I closed my eyes and prayed. Opening them, I noticed *the ceiling light above me had turned on!* The Lord is indeed here comforting me all the time.

May 7, 1985 –

Last Saturday we attended the opera. My hands became warm during the performance. At intermission, we went out to the hall and a man with his arm in a sling came and stood nearby. I was moved to asked about his arm. He seemed to be in great pain and said he had broken his shoulder an automobile accident and could not find a way to get comfortable. I prayed silently for his healing and his pain. His face immediately relaxed and the next intermission he was laughing and talking to everyone.

May 14, 1985 —

We are at Casper, Wyoming, on the second day of our trip to Alaska. At nine there is still deep dusk. Soon it will be light until late. Driving today, I watched scenery most of the time. It was brilliant and beautiful—almost unbelievably so.

One night recently we watched "The A Team" on television. Later, the Spirit seemed to be absent when I said my evening prayers. I confessed my sin and the next morning these words came from the Lord: "My kingdom does not consist in violence to people" (see Mt 5:39).

No matter what happened to the Jews and others during the Holocaust, God did not intend it, but allowed it for his own reasons. He did not ordain it.

I started getting tense today on our journey and suffered a bladder flare-up and a swollen neck gland. The Lord sent the hymn: "Drop thy still dew of quietness till all our strivings cease; take from our souls the strain and stress, and let our ordered lives confess the beauty of thy peace." During the next few days, I followed this advice and recovery came fast.

May 19, 1985 —

Last night I had a strange dream. Beth was back from heaven, sitting at my kitchen table, tenderly working with her husband at a game of some sort. [Hal had Alzheimer's disease at the time, and still does.] I asked her how she got here and she replied she'd asked to come. She said heaven is harder to get into than one would think.

May 20, 1985 –

I was reading 2 Chronicles today about King Solomon's building of the temple. When the temple was completed, a great holiday celebration took place. Solomon said a prayer of dedication and the temple was filled with the glory of God. Solomon also prayed that the Lord would teach the people, *the good way in which they should walk* (6:27). God desires order and created order in the universe and on earth. The Lord wants us to have order in our lives—not chaos, anarchy, hedonism.

Solomon also mentioned the Israelites as a people—a community. The nation was to be rewarded or punished as a whole, not as solitary individuals. This is where the individualism of 20th century America is going astray. This everyone-for-themselves mind-set is causing us to lose the blessing of God.

May 26, 1985 –

We drove the camper onto a ferry at Prince Rupert, British Columbia, disembarking at Petersburg, Alaska—our first visit to Alaska.

Today we attended a Lutheran church and as we sat there, my palms became warmed with the Spirit, so I knew the Lord was present in that place. The pastor came down to our pew and invited us to their annual picnic. We felt welcome, so we went. The food was delicious and all the congregation took turns coming to talk to us. We watched the children race and play games. It was a good day.

Christians are the same everywhere—friendly to strangers, unselfish, kind, concerned with goodness and order—and demonstrating the love of God.

June 6, 1985 –

I am reading St. *Innocent, Apostle to America* by Paul Garrett which tells the story of an Eastern Orthodox missionary priest sent to Alaska when this land still belonged to Russia. This is an excellent source of religious history of Alaska. As in Roman Catholicism, many truths of Orthodoxy can be sources of inspiration:

1. The long elaborate robes and stoles worn by priests are not for their glorification but are visual reminders of the glory of God, so are as valid for this purpose as fancy cathedrals, stained glass windows, religious paintings, sculpture or sacred music. Whatever helps inspire awe in the congregation is a legitimate religious symbol.

2. The incense burned during worship is a reminder of the "odor of a sweet smell" (Phil 4:18) that comes occasionally to people when the Holy Spirit is near.

3. This great apostle, St. Innocent, was asked, "If God is infinitely merciful, how can the Lord deprive anyone of his heavenly kingdom?" He replied, "The same reason you keep twisting your head back and forth to avoid sun in your eyes. God doesn't deprive sinners who don't repent of his heavenly kingdom, they themselves simply cannot bear its light – anymore than you can bear the light of the sun."

4. A member of a very primitive tribe, ministered to by this priest, seemed to catch truth from God faster than many other more sophisticated people. A tribe member explained, "Tungus always pray. Tungus know God give all. If I just kill one partridge, I know it's God who give all things. If I don't make kill, I know it's because God not give me anything. This mean I bad and so I pray to God."

5. St. Innocent frequently blessed waters around villages and led processions of the faithful in a march around their church or chapel singing and praying.

6. The Eastern Orthodox faithful believe that God is in control of history so following God's plan and living

under the Lord's jurisdiction will bring joy, happiness and peace; not doing frequently causes the opposite.

7. The Orthodox faithful believe their task is to Christianize the world.

8. St. Innocent operated on the truth of the verse, Psalms 37:23, *Our steps are made firm by the Lord, when he delights in our way.* This means everyone should be unconditionally obedient to God's will in every incident in our lives. Amen!

9. On Easter morning St. Innocent called on every member of his local church announcing, "Christ is risen!"

June 9, 1985 —

Today Howard rested while I visited a small Anglican church in Haines Junction, Yukon Territory. There were 14 people there: five tribal members, two women visiting from England, three young women from another town, three members of the congregation and myself.

The young deacon is to be ordained this week. He conducted a Pentecost service because he was gone two weeks ago. The Spirit was powerfully present throughout the service and I went forward for Communion.

At the back of the church stood a squat stove and near it stood a playpen for babies and toddlers. There were pews for a couple dozen people. The altar was covered with a beautiful white leather drape embroidered with church symbols. A wheezy organ filled one corner and whenever the organist played, the priest frowned. He led prayers for the Queen of England—a new experience for me.

We stopped by the same church on the way home. The priest told us they had allowed transients to sleep in the church until one bunch of hippies burned all the prayer books and hymnals. He also said they held healing services every Friday evening and the church was growing because of it.

June 25, 1985 —

Yesterday we went to a Laundromat. The woman on duty was young, blond and pretty—but something was troubling her. I don't remember who spoke first, but it was friend at first sight. Soon she was telling me of a boyfriend who was supposed to marry her but was now resisting. She felt they had made a big mistake living together for three years. I told her to pray for the solution to the problem and to ask for the Lord's help. I told her I would pray for her also. She said she had been praying and the Lord had told her to go see her minister, but she hadn't gone. I told her to obey the word of the Lord. We talked a long time and when we left, I hugged her. I'm certain the Lord arranged this visit.

June 27, 1985 —

What a glorious day! A boat ride in Resurrection Bay rewarded us with sightings of seals, sea lions, otters and thousands of gulls and murres. We also viewed cormorants, puffins and murrelets—bird species we had never seen before. The sun was shining; it was warm and we rejoiced.

The Lord has been with us every day and all is going well. The sun shone when we have gone out in boats to see and photograph birds; the Lord has healed several small medical needs of ours and God has brought peace in this camper when tempers flared. Not a day goes by that I don't discover some way God has helped us. Today the Lord knew we didn't want to kill the bee that was in the camper, so he caused it to light on the fly swatter so I could carry it to the door.

It has occurred to me that when the Lord brings something about that is not a natural event, he does not suspend the natural law, but supersedes it—almost like breaking into the physical world briefly with a spiritual truth made visible by being made physical.

June 28, 1985 —

The anointing with oil that I have done during this trip has kept the camper going fine. Whenever a problem arises, I anoint that spot with oil. My bottle of holy oil, made holy by being in the presence of the Holy Spirit during fervent prayer, is not running dry, even though I gave away half of it and have used it often. Thank you, God.

July 19, 1985 —

A week ago we flew to St. Paul Island in the Pribilofs to photograph puffins. Every day the tour bus took us on another adventure on this tiny island, four by fourteen-miles long. We managed to observe and photograph cliffs of sea birds, lovely wild flowers and fur seals—all exhilarating and beautiful.

One day Howard and I were driven and deposited at the stone quarry in the middle of the island. We climbed to a high rock overlooking the terrain, then sat watching and listening. It was foggy and very quiet. Occasionally a snow bunting or rosy finch or lapland longspur would wing by.

As the clouds rolled in off the Bering Sea we became enveloped in almost complete silence. We felt totally isolated and yet at peace. What wonderful experiences we are having! The Lord is traveling with us, intercepting all trouble and blessing us with awesome views of God's lovely world. The Lord is showing us the beauty he has created and prepared for his children.

I discovered the Lord had a job for me in Alaska. We met a retired couple from Iowa visiting the Pribilofs to observe fur seals. We didn't know until the last day that the husband, Carroll, was losing his eyesight. Immediately I wondered how

I could put my hands on him and pray. Would he accept this? His wife did not want him to know she had told us about his affliction so I couldn't go to him directly.

The last morning, he mentioned how sore his eyes felt from overuse. This gave me an opening and the Lord provided the time and place because Carroll was alone on the bus when I got on. I moved quickly, telling him I had success in calling down God's healing power for people, and asked if I could put my hands on his eyes and pray. He readily agreed. I proceeded, asking aloud for God to heal his eyes in Jesus' name. I asked him if he had faith in God, and he said yes. I will write him later to check on his eyes.

July 29, 1985 –

Today we drove 130 miles north of Fairbanks on a dirt road. The dust was fierce and the road was deteriorating, so we turned back before reaching the Yukon River, stopping at a mountain area of high tundra where we walked a while. A family group of rock ptarmigans stepped across our path and juvenile surfbirds were thick in the area. Strange that surfbirds, which spend their entire lives on rocky coasts, withdraw to inland tundra to nest.

We came upon a view point where we could see 75 miles in every direction with no trees in sight. It was an impressive feeling to know we were almost on top of the world, so to speak. I could empathize with the sailors in Columbus' crew who worried about falling off the world. Though I knew better in my mind, my instinct said, "We've gone too far."

All day long we felt the Lord's presence. Once we stopped to give assistance to a stranded motorist and almost got into trouble. When he sauntered over to the camper and looked at us, I observed in his eyes a soul-less, conscience-less quality. Terror rose in me and I wondered if we were going to be robbed and murdered. I was already praying when Howard asked him if he needed help. Abruptly, the man turned on his heel and walked away as though he had seen something in our camper he didn't like. I said to Howard, "Go quickly," and we did. Later that day on our way back to Fairbanks, we did not see him or his two equally evil-looking companions.

July 31, 1985 —

Tonight, we are back camping in Haines Junction, 800 miles south of the northern-most point we visited. It is quiet except for the twittering of swallows. I walked down to the Anglican church to pray and get a photograph. The priest was there, so we had a nice talk and discovered we had a great deal in common. I wished him God's blessings and prayed for him later.

August 7, 1985 —

We are at Prince George, British Columbia. It was a hard, rough, slow, stressful drive down the Cassiar Highway. Tension built up for several days and by yesterday I was completely unstrung. For a time, I felt utterly alone, abandoned by God and unable to reach him. I even wondered for my sanity, but tonight before dark I was hiking alone in the woods near the campground when I reached a clearing and looked up to see a beautiful complete rainbow. It said to me that God is always true and near and will never abandon us. Praise him! I feel much better.

September 21, 1985 —

I am sitting in my prayer closet at home in peace and quiet, catching up with myself. I attended Ed O'Rourke's funeral today. He was 97. When the congregation sang the hymn, "Be Not Afraid," I almost became unglued, crying with an intensity I hadn't experienced for years. In it was sadness for the passing of a great old man, release of tension I have felt with Howard's retirement, his surgery during the past month, sorrow for the loss of friendship with two very dear old friends and sadness that Ann and Clyde are leaving town.

I went to see Dad at the nursing home this afternoon, as I do every day. Driving home, it occurred to me that it would be comforting to see an angel, as Roland Buck did in his book, *Angels on Assignment.*

I turned on the car radio to hear a minister speaking words of reassurance that seemed spoken directly to me: "When you have problems and griefs and stresses that seem to overpower you, remember Jesus lived through all those problems too, and so did the prophets and Peter and Paul and others. You are not suffering anything that Jesus didn't experience in some way. He is here now to help you through the toughest problems. Just give yourself to him and he will be with you and help you."

Abruptly, he finished, and unrelated music came on with no explanation. Where did this sermon come from? The Lord is listening to my mind and helping me to make it across the muddy ditches. Praise him!

I have asked for the gift of tongues and pray aloud at times thinking it may come. Once this week my flesh began to tingle and my tongue thickened but no words emerged in tongues.

September 26, 1985 –

The same way a thin layer of Spirit separated my flesh from the stings of fire ants in Florida, so will a thin layer of the same Spirit protect my heart and mind from any blow, regardless of where it originates or who attacks or how powerful the assault may be. This message arrived this morning from the Lord and can be found in Psalm 91. I am already being protected and know it. Praise God!

I stepped out of the camper the other night into thin air, having forgotten to lower the steps. Though I grabbed the door frame while falling, I still hit the ground pretty hard. I sang out several times, "Praise the Lord," remembering the string trimmer episode. Then I got up, dusted myself off and went in the house. No pain, no after effects, no bruises. How good this wonderful Lord of the Universe is!

October 6, 1985 –

Last week, Mary Bowman left the Bible study class in the middle of the lesson with heart palpitations and extreme angina pain. The class prayed for her, then I slipped out and went to the sanctuary where she was lying down on a pew. I knelt beside her, held her and prayed aloud that the Lord would heal her ailing heart. I spoke softly to her, telling her not ever to be afraid, recited the 23rd Psalm and the Lord's Prayer to calm her and then a short prayer of healing. The pain subsided and she sat up and said she was all right. I phoned her today and she was fine, the doctor had changed the medicine and she feels better. But it was the Lord who healed her. Thank you, Lord.

I woke up earlier this week singing a funeral hymn. I wondered if Dad might be ill, so we went to him immediately. He was experiencing heart pain from congestive heart failure and was near death. With modern medications, the doctor soon had his heart back under control, and he seemed to be all right later in the day. Perhaps the Lord will allow him to live to see his 93rd birthday next February.

October 28, 1985 —

We just heard the exciting news that Mae Robinson, the daughter of a friend, has been miraculously healed of multiple sclerosis. She was sitting in a chair praying when a net of light entered the room and covered her. She was immediately healed. The M.S. lesions on the brain that were apparent on the X ray are now gone. Many were praying for her, including me. She knows God healed her, and her faith is strong. Praise the Lord!

November 2, 1985 —

I have been praying the Lord Jesus would enter my being in such a way that I would experience the kind of love he has for people, particularly those who are hard to love.

November 11, 1985 —

This week I have been praying for Belle, a paralyzed 50-year-old woman in the nursing home who has tubes in her nose for feeding and breathing. Today I was there and saw Belle with the tubes removed, eating and talking! Another miracle! Praise God! Her husband said she had been improving all week.

November 15, 1985 —

I have been very busy with *things* this week and have not taken time to pray and meditate adequately. For the past two days, I have been hearing a hymn, "Jesus is Tenderly Calling Today." Does it mean Dad is dying or is the message for me? Last night in my prayer closet, the Spirit was only faintly present. I searched myself for sin but couldn't think of any big ones. Then I remembered telling Howard yesterday that our church has members who speak in tongues, but I don't. The tone of my voice was relief. However, I have asked the Lord for that gift. I was vacillating and the Lord knew it.

This morning I looked out the window at the damp earth. We've had three days of heavy rain and I thought about Elijah not finding God in rain or wind or earthquake, but in a still small voice. After breakfast I retired to the bedroom with the Bible and looked up the Elijah passage. It opened to 1 Kings 18. *Elijah then came near to all the people, and said, "How long will you go limping with two different opinions?"* (v. 21).

So the Lord's silence last night was because of my denial of him to Howard yesterday. I asked forgiveness and the Spirit returned. Perhaps the Lord plans to send me the gift of tongues or the gift of prophecy. I am totally unworthy but maybe I can grow in the Lord and he will allow me this honor. Praise him!

December 14, 1985 –

I have been talking and listening to the Lord at night when it is very quiet. I wake up early, refreshed and mentally alert. There are answers, but I am not certain if what I am hearing is from him or only my imagination. One day I woke up singing, "He lives, he lives; I know my Savior lives; he walks with me and talks with me..." At least some answers are from him. I asked if humankind would be allowed to destroy the earth.

He said, "People start wars, *but I am in control of the earth.*" Then I remembered the Psalms: *By the word of the Lord the heavens were made, and all their host by the breath of his mouth. He gathered the waters of the sea as in a bottle; he put the deeps in storehouses. Let all the earth fear the Lord; let all the inhabitants of the world stand in awe of him. For he spoke, and it came to be; he commanded, and it stood firm* (33:6-9). I asked about the earthquake in Mexico—why had God allowed it to happen and hurt and kill so many innocent people, including young children. There was a vague feeling that I couldn't understand the answer to at first. Then a definite response came: "Pain cannot harm the soul." I understood that. Pain cannot basically harm a person's character. *"Do not fear those who kill the body but cannot kill the soul; rather fear him who can destroy both soul and body in hell. Are not two sparrows sold for a penny? Yet not one of them will fall to the ground apart from your Father. And even the hairs of your head are all counted. So do not be afraid; you are of more value than many sparrows. Everyone therefore who acknowledges me before others, I also will acknowledge before my Father in heaven; but whoever denies me before others, I will also deny before my Father in heaven"* (Mt 10:28-33).

December 22, 1985 —

I made a large vat of chili Friday for our annual Audubon gathering after the mid-winter bird census. When I tasted it, the cumin taste was too heavy, making it bitter. I anointed the pan with holy oil and put it out in the garage to cool. When I heated and tasted it Saturday night, it was good! *Praise the Lord!* I hesitated to ask the Lord to do this, then he reminded me that he had changed water to wine at a wedding party (Jn 2:1-10). How good God is!

Last week, I began preparing for the Sunday school party at our house. I bought an artificial Christmas tree and set it in the corner of the living room undecorated. That night, the Lord said, "Get rid of that tree."

I said, "I just bought it."

"Get rid of it."

"Why?"

"What does it mean?"

"Life, joy of Christmas, warm memories, love."

"What does the tree itself stand for?"

"I suppose you are talking about Wotan, the old German god who was supposed to live in it."

"Exactly, so get it out of the house," the Lord said.

I lay awake several hours that night pondering this conversation. I have always loved trees—climbed them constantly until I was 15 years old and finally stopped to avoid embarrassing my mother.

Our maple tree was my favorite; I could climb higher in it that any other. I even hung by the knees from one of the higher limbs until Dad saw me one day and scolded me. We made whistles from that maple tree. If you cut a four-inch twig at the right time of year, slip the bark off, cut slits in the wood, and slip the bark back on, you can make a dandy whistle. The same tree served as a hideout when pirates or cattle rustlers were about.

The thing I remember best about that particular maple tree was learning from it that the world is round. As I perched high in a crotch, I could watch Dad walk behind the horses, plowing the field on top of the hill. And as he plowed, he slowly disappeared over the hill. To my mind, he was walking over the arc of the earth's great circle.

Walnut trees down in the bottoms provided a source of Christmas income for the neighbor boy and me. On a November day, our mothers would send us out with picnic lunches, a small hand-pulled wagon and gunny sacks to put walnuts in. Having little sense of the passage of time, Bobby and I would collect the walnuts, eat our lunches and be back home before noon. We would then hull the walnuts by dumping them in the gravel driveway so cars would run over them and then sell walnuts for a few pennies a bag. We were awarded with a wonderful sense of accomplishment.

One of the big fallen trees in the bottoms provided logs for a raft Bobby and I built. It took my brother's help with the team of horses to drag those logs to the little creek—a small, narrow spring and run-off waterway which was backed up by a low-water dam. All our free hours one summer were spent poling up and down that creek with ocean storms or river rapids or jungle streams coursing past. The persimmon trees on the hillside were also part of my childhood. I remember the day I climbed one to pick some luscious looking persimmons. Alas! I can still taste the mouth-puckering unripe fruit. Pretty persimmons, round and orange, are not ripe. You have to wait until they get ugly and wrinkled and spotted to be edible.

Christmas trees were special. My dad would pick up one on sale the day before Christmas and my sister and I would decorate it until we were certain it was the most beautiful tree we had ever seen. Why, everyone in the United States had a Christmas tree—almost everyone in the world! Christmas trees had become popular world wide—not nativity scenes with sheep and donkeys and angels and baby Jesus. *Oh, I see!* I got up and chucked the tree out the back door, went back to bed, and slept peacefully.

The next morning I felt the Spirit of God warming my entire body. I had to throw off my covers. The heat lasted almost an hour. After that, I got up and anointed the whole house.

I am continuing to receive messages from the Lord through Scripture and songs. The day we were having a family crisis at home, the Bible opened to 1 Corinthians 13—Paul's love poem.

December 23, 1985 –

For a month now, I have been thinking about suggesting to the Monday prayer group we go pray for sick children in the hospital. My thoughts have not been organized enough to decide how to start, but at two this morning God said to me, "Dottie, you are in charge of going to the hospital to pray for the children. Go, and I will tell you what to do."

"When, Lord?"

"Tomorrow."

"Christmas Eve?"

"Yes."

December 25, 1985 —

Yesterday, we were in the middle of lunch when the Lord said, "Go now." I told Howard I was going to the hospital to pray for someone.

He said, "Who?"

I said, "I don't know."

He looked at me strangely but has learned not to question some of the odd things I do, so off I went.

Walking down the long hospital hallway to the elevator I wondered how to find the children's wing since I didn't have a name to look for. While I was in the corridor, a woman dressed as a nurse marched toward me and stopped in front of me. I asked her where to find the children's ward and she said it was on the sixth floor tower and then described in detail how to get there.

The first thing I did on arrival was circle the hallway to see if any children were there before settling in the waiting room to pray. There seemed to be patients in two rooms, but before I could make a decision about which one to enter, a nurse stopped me and asked who I was looking for. Embarrassed, I said I was looking for the sixth floor waiting room. She replied, "You passed it to get here."

I thanked her, then hurried back to the waiting room and sat down. I started praying for those two children and any other children who might be here. Then I prayed for the whole hospital of sick and injured people. When my hands cooled, I paused and looked up. Seeing the decorated Christmas tree in the room, I decided to pray for the removal of all evil from the hospital. At that, my hands became very warm again. So I ordered out, in Jesus' name, all evil spirits and asked God to post angels at all the doors and windows. Then I asked that an angel band march down every hallway and into every room singing Glory to God and Psalms.

As I prayed this, I visualized it. Then, my hands cooled off and I stopped. I said, "Is that it, Lord?'

He said, "Wait."

Pretty soon, a gray lady volunteer came along so I stopped her and asked her to find out if there were any sick children. I said, "It may seem strange to you, but the Lord asked me to come here and pray for sick children."

She said, "No, it doesn't seem strange to me at all. I am a Lutheran and we pray for the sick."

She came back to the waiting room later and said there were only two patients, mentioning the rooms they were in. I prayed not to be stopped by a nurse, walked to the first room and entered. By then the Lord had taken over and I was bold.

A woman was sitting at the bedside—not a fair-haired, fresh-faced, thriving young woman—but someone who looked as though life had dealt harshly with her. I told her the Lord had sent me to pray for her baby. She looked startled but said okay. I walked to the crib and looked at a four-month-old baby whose head was badly bruised. He was whimpering. My hands were burning by then, so I put my left hand lightly on the middle of his back and started praying aloud. I actually *felt the heat from my hand drain down into that baby!*

I prayed in Jesus' name that he would be filled with the resurrection healing of Christ and would grow up to be a healthy, happy person who would be a credit to his parents, his community and to God. He stopped whimpering and slept. I turned to his mother, comforted her, and as I left she was weeping.

The child next door lay under an oxygen tent so I thought it best not to go in further or touch him. I knelt in the doorway and prayed a silent prayer of healing, then left the hospital, greatly rejoicing. Obedience to the Lord, no matter what the cost, brings unspeakable joy. I had faith those two children would be healed by the power of God in Christ. My feet did not touch the floor all the way to the car. Praise God!

December 26, 1985 –

The Lord said, "You are to read the Bible daily; study my word carefully." This song came to mind today, "Lead me, Lord; lead me in thy righteousness; *make thy way plain before my face* ... "

January 1, 1986 –

A most wonderful event occurred last night. I have been reading, *Nine O'clock in the Morning,* by Dennis Bennett which is the story of his receiving the spiritual gift of tongues. As I said evening prayers on my knees, I asked for that gift. After I went to bed, my body started getting warm with the Spirit, my lips quivered, and my tongue became thick. I opened my mouth and started speaking something which came from deep inside me. Out came a most beautiful language, unknown to me. It was within my control as to *whether or not* I would speak it, but what came from my lips was not of my doing. I had received the spiritual gift of tongues after two years of trying. I found out today that Jenny happened to be praying *at that very moment* for me to receive this gift.

Not wanting to waken Howard, I spoke in a whisper. Then I put on a robe and retired to another room where the Spirit language continued for about an hour. I thought through my list of people and situations to pray for, and my tone and verbiage changed each time I changed thoughts. I knew the Spirit was praying for me or through me. Hallelujah! Now the Spirit will be more easily released to heal the people I pray for. Jesus really does the healing. I merely ask in his name.

Today I began singing, "O Lord, most merciful, O Lord, most holy; almighty Father, we would still be praising always." Joy is so close to me most of the time. I have a feeling Beth is working on this from her station in heaven. Thanks to her and praise to God!

The neighbor family next door has become involved in a Baptist church. I had asked their son Raymond to come to Sunday school with me and he declined. Since then I have been praying for them. God intervened to get them to church. "God is so good; God is so good; He's so good to me." Praise him!

January 4, 1986 –

We are at Falcon State Park, Texas on the Rio Grande River, basking in warm sunshine in our shirt-sleeves. We had made arrangements for someone to look after Dad's laundry and other needs and had promised to call every other day. So with a free heart, we set out, I in the Toyota following Howard in our mini-motor home of advanced age. One of the charms of this spot so close to the border is seeing rare Mexican birds that stray across the river. When we come here we always put out seeds near the camper and photograph all the desert birds that come to feed.

January 14, 1986 –

While resting and unwinding from all the travel tension, I have been reading Hebrews in two different versions. Particularly striking is the faith chapter—eleven. Since the Lord required me to throw away the Christmas tree and said he was testing my faith and obedience, I have thought a lot about Abraham.

The Lord tested Abraham by asking him to sacrifice his son, then released him from that request by furnishing the ram on the mountain. When Abraham fulfilled that faith test, God chose his descendants through whom to speak to humankind. What powerful faith Abraham had! All this makes sense except *what* God requested him to do.

My logic says God wouldn't ask Abraham to kill his son, but I know my logic and God's logic are not the same. However, I am asking God to speak to me about this problem. Several truths come to mind:

1. God *spoke* to Abraham.
2. Abraham heard God's voice.
3. Abraham was absolutely certain that he was hearing the God who created him and all that is.
4. Abraham trusted the voice and the power or person behind the voice.
5. Abraham loved God and wanted to obey him.
6. Abraham was strong enough to obey God even in the most adverse circumstances – and continued to love and respect God.
7. Abraham obeyed God's voice rather than his own logic.
8. Abraham chose God over family.

9. Abraham was not afraid.
10. Abraham rested the night before leaving home to carry out God's command. *So Abraham rose early in the morning, and took two of his young men with him, and Isaac his son ...* (Gen 22:3).

Shortly after writing about my problem in God's test of Abraham, the Bible opened in my hand to Job 38:4, 12 *"Where were you when I laid the foundation of the earth? Tell me, if you have understanding ... Have you commanded the morning since your days began, and caused the dawn to know its place?"* The Lord is telling me God knows his own business and who am I to question? Amen.

January 16, 1986 –

The Lord God is in control of this world and all worlds. He has told me this. I am beginning to understand how close God is to all creatures including me. Whenever I think of God, he is nearby. I'm certain when I am not thinking of God, he is also nearby.

I attended a little Baptist church at Falcon Heights soon after we arrived in South Texas. There were fewer than a dozen people at Sunday school and only 15 in attendance at church. A man in Sunday school suggested we pray for the other churches we pass on our way through town. I then suggested we also pray for every family in this Baptist church and for the church. So I did all week. The next Sunday, there were 18 at Sunday school and 50 at church. We are leaving here shortly, but I will continue to pray for them.

January 20, 1986 –

This morning early, the Lord sent the hymn, "Softly and tenderly, Jesus is calling ... "

I said, "Yes, Lord."

God replied, "You have not done what I asked. You need to rest, drink lots of water, eat lightly and pray continually." So today I did just that. For several days I have not felt well and have been asking the Lord to send healing.

While resting today, I mentioned to the Lord, "Is Beth where you can reach her with a message?"

He said, "You bet!"

I said, "Will you tell her how much joy I am having and about the gift of the Spirit I received?"

Almost before I got it out, the answer came, "She knows."

January 23, 1986—

Something happened yesterday that is so strange I almost hesitate to put it down—but it is too marvelous to keep secret. Walking alone on a Santa Ana National Wildlife Refuge trail, I stepped off the trail to see a little bird and in the process brushed hard against a cactus. The spines penetrated my jeans, heavy wool socks, light polypropylene sock and into my leg. Pulling out the thorns, I noticed the thin polypropylene sock had two holes in it with an inch-long run. I thought at the time Howard would be angry because I had borrowed them from him without asking. When I returned to camp and took off the sock, the polypropylene one was *completely whole*—absolutely perfect—no holes where they had been! Marvelous! Praise God who does wondrous works for those who try to obey him and love him and have faith in him! He has told me to expect rewards for some things I do. How can I ever live up to his gifts?

January 26, 1986—

Personal worship last night was good. I sat alone in the Toyota and at first the Spirit did not seem to be present, so I wept.

What could I have said or done to drive away the Spirit? Then the Spirit came rushing in, and it was a wonderful, worshipful experience. I prayed for many things—the world and people everywhere. Our near neighbors here in the campground were having a noisy row, so I prayed fervently for them. I ended asking for the baptism of the Holy Spirit again and burst into song in tongues. It was a tune in a minor key and the words sounded Jewish. When I came back to the camper, the Bible opened to Revelation 21:2-4: *"And I saw the holy city, the new Jerusalem, coming down out of heaven from God, prepared as a bride adorned for her husband. And I heard a loud voice from the throne saying, 'See, the home of God is among mortals. He will dwell with them as their God; they will be his peoples, and God himself will be with them; **he will wipe every tear from their eyes**. Death will be no more; mourning and crying and pain will be no more, for the first things have passed away.' "*

This morning upon awakening, I thanked God for this earth, telling the Lord how much I loved it and all the creatures and everything in it. The hymn, "How Great Thou Art," immediately came to mind and I relished in the words, "O Lord my God! when I in awesome wonder, consider all the worlds thy hands have made, I see the stars, I hear the rolling thunder, thy power throughout the universe displayed. Then sings my soul, my Savior God to thee; how great thou art! ..."

I have been asking the Lord how to be certain of his voice. Tonight I read Jeremiah 23:29, *Is not my word like fire, says the Lord, and like a hammer that breaks a rock in pieces?*

I have increasingly become aware that the Lord is asking me to give my witness to a dear Jewish friend, Sandra. Various Bible passages telling of God's concern for Jews have recently impressed themselves on me and Sunday the Lord sent me to a church where it seemed the message was directed to me personally. It was the call of the Lord in Jeremiah 1:7-8, *"For you shall go to all to whom I send you, and you shall speak whatever I command you. Do not be afraid of them, for I am with you to deliver you," says the Lord.* So I wrote Sandra four pages and was at peace, but didn't mail it. That night the Lord told me I hadn't included in it that Jesus died for our sins. So I rewrote that part and mailed it. Afterward, the Lord said, "Well done, good and faithful servant."

February 6, 1986 —

Today I became aware that Sandra had received the letter and blew up. Last night I was so tired I could hardly think straight—more tired than I can remember being for a long time. My sensitivity to messages from the Lord has laid me open to receive messages in my spirit from people also. I worried that I shouldn't have written it, but am receiving the Lord's confirmation that I did right.

The Lord called my attention to Romans 10:1-15, *Brothers and sisters, my heart's desire and prayer to God for them is that they may be saved. I can testify that they have a zeal for God, but it is not enlightened. ... But how are they to call on one in whom they have not believed? And how are they to believe in one of whom they have never heard? And how are they to hear without someone to proclaim him? And how are they to proclaim him unless they are sent?*

February 14, 1986 —

This morning I woke very early to a hymn the Lord was sending. "Jesus is calling; Oh, lis't to his voice."

I said, "Yes, Lord." Then came the message:

1. Dad will pass on this spring. I asked if he would be accepted by God and the answer was yes, Dad would be sent to where he could be taught what he needs to know.

2. The Lord said not to mention these things to anyone. All this was accompanied by a tremendously warm surge through my entire body which lasted more than an hour.

February 15, 1986 —

Today while driving, I turned on the radio and heard Dr. James Kennedy from Coral Ridge Presbyterian Church in Florida, narrate a parable with such an impact it almost knocked me out of the seat. He told of a man who was visiting a family one evening. There was a knock and five officers of the law entered, arrested and bound the visitor and carried him off to prison. So much evidence was brought against him in the trial that he was convicted and sentenced to death. The father of the family he was visiting went to the judge to see if he could do something for his friend because he loved him. The judge said his friend had to die for all the crimes he had committed; justice required it. The father then offered himself in place of the convicted one, but the judge refused, saying that was not enough sacrifice for the convicted one had done many criminal and immoral acts. He then asked the father if he had childre. The father admitted he had a son, 17, who was his pride and joy. To this the judge replied that the son would be the acceptable substitute.

After discussion with the son which involved tremendous emotional distress on both parts, the father brought his son and handed him over to the judge. The judge then said, "Oh, no, we can't do it; you must do it. That's the only way the sacrifice would be enough to cancel all the terrible crimes your friend has committed." So with great anguish of heart, the father bound his son, strapped him in, and pulled the switch. The boy, in his last act, looked shocked, terrified and disbelieving as he squirmed in agony and died. The criminal went free.

This story had such a powerful impact on me, my lips quivered and I broke into tongues of prayer. I thought back on Abraham who essentially had done this very act, except for a last minute reprieve. I thought of that hapless man and all the anguish he went through knowing what he had to do and prepared to do it. I thought of Isaac as he looked at his father in horror and dismay, and of Abraham having to see this expression on the face of his only and beloved and long-awaited son.

Here, finally, is the answer to the problem of God's requiring Abraham to sacrifice his son. *No other test* would be enough to show Abraham's abiding love and trust of God.

February 22, 1986 —

Yesterday I woke with the message that the Lord wished me to go to the hospital and pray for Elias or Ellis. In the hospital notes of the newspaper was listed a newborn boy Ellis. At the most inconvenient time, the Lord said, "Now." Starting for the hospital, I still wondered if it were all my imagination.

I said, "Lord, send me a sign. Give me a parking place next to the door." *There was.* I went inside and tried to call Jenny to tell her I would be late for our luncheon date. No answer. I sat down in the lobby to listen for further instructions. Before I could get very far into prayer, a friend who had a need came by and started a long conversation. All was lost. I would not be able to hear the Lord's instructions and/or keep my agreement to meet Jenny. After the conversation finished, I walked to the desk and asked about the baby Ellis. He and his mother were discharged this morning, the registrar said. I walked out slowly.

Then I remembered meeting a woman carrying a newborn baby out as I was coming in. Could they have been the ones?

Somehow I felt at peace as though the errand had been completed. Perhaps when I prayed for that mother and baby as I passed them coming in, the assignment had been fulfilled. Arriving at the cafe, I sat quietly in the car and said a little prayer. From somewhere came, "Well done, good and faithful servant."

March 7, 1986 —

My friend Jenny said angels attend us at all times and also that many of them have wings. Last night at bedtime, I was thinking about angels, so I asked to see one. In the night, a sound awakened me. Opening my eyes, I saw nothing. Then I became aware of activity around me—like moving vapors or shadows. A great deal of movement was going on in that room, but I didn't see anything identifiable.

March 8, 1986 —

Last night I awakened in the middle of the night, kept my eyes closed and asked, "Is the angel here?"

"Yes."

"What is your name?"

"Amarsa."

"Are there many like you?"

"Yes."

"Why can't I see you?" I had opened my eyes and looked.

"You are afraid to see me."

"Will I see you someday?"

"Yes, when you aren't afraid."

My body and hands felt warm with the Spirit so I knew these manifestations were of God, not Satan.

March 9, 1986—

Again last night I awakened. We had been to the opera and it was after midnight when we went to bed. Waking a little later, I was not aware of anything spiritual in the room; however, I asked if the angel Amarsa were there. An answer came that the name is *Amersa,* not Amarsa. I said, if you are here, make a noise. The bedroom door banged pretty loudly, but, alas, I was too tired to think of anything to ask. I went to sleep.

Today the Lord sent a song, "Rescue the perishing; pray for the dying." The phrase, "pray for the dying" kept repeating over and over, so I went to the prayer closet and prayed a general prayer of mercy and grace for all who were dying, lifting them in my prayers to the arms of Jesus. I kept at that prayer all afternoon. Then the words of the end of the song came to me with renewed emphasis, "Jesus is merciful; Jesus will save." So I knew that the prayers had been heard and answered.

March 10, 1986—

Meg called today and said that Gary, the son of a friend living in a nearby city, is seriously ill with multiple sclerosis and is almost blind and paralyzed. This news was so upsetting I have been praying long and fervently for him ever since. Tonight the Bible opened to several healing passages in Matthew, chiefly the centurion's servant's healing at a distance (8:5-13). I am wondering if this message is about Gary or Marilyn, my sister's friend in Missouri. Or both.

March 11, 1986—

Yesterday as I drove down the street, I prayed for the sick that I knew about and asked that they be made a part of my spiritual family, then claimed them for Christ. Immediately, I turned on the radio to a Christian station. Someone was singing a song with lyrics, "It's only a matter of mercy; only a matter of grace ... that I'm a member of the family of God." I knew this was an answer from the Lord. Thank you, Lord.

March 21, 1986 –

The Lord sent a message today by way of a radio program that all life is sacred, including that of malformed and retarded children. One should deal with such children with the grace and love of Christ in our hearts—this is expected of Christians. Then the Lord sent the song "Ave Maria" to my mind and I realized I am to deal with the problems with Dad, both present and future, as a Christian mother deals with troublesome, difficult children and I would be sent grace to cope.

March 26, 1986, 4:25 a.m. –

The Lord said to get up, he had some messages for me. "I desire that you know me and my power to heal. Remove all distractions, and listen with your whole heart. You need to fast and you will hear me better. Be to me a witness to all you meet or come in contact with. Be my light to the world. Pray and praise without ceasing."

The Lord said not to be concerned about the future—to leave it to him and not to worry about it.

April 4, 1986–

We are at Big Bend National Park for a few days. In the shade with a breeze it is comfortable. At night it cools nicely. Before five this morning the Lord awakened me, "Get up."

I said, "What for?"

"I'm going to show you my comet."

After lying there a couple more minutes, I got up and went

out. From the moment I stepped out the door, I felt as though every step were directed by God. He told me to orient my directions with the Big Dipper and the North Star. Then I walked the road until the view of the south was clear of trees. The Milky Way was obvious, so with binoculars I started scanning the southern end of the Milky Way and *there was Halley's Comet*—20° above the horizon and adjacent to the Milky Way. I saw a thick fuzzy star with tail pointed to the right and up a little from the horizontal. The comet was not visible without binoculars. I praised and thanked God and went back to bed. How exciting to have the Lord of the Universe as a friend!

Yesterday we stopped for gasoline at a small town in Texas. An old man, putting gas in his jalopy beside us, was eager to talk to us. He was about 70 years old, in overalls, with a wrinkled and rather weathered face. He had been shot in World War II and was also injured in an industrial accident. We talked about the weather and he told us about roads and towns around there. In all, he smiled a crooked smile and was very friendly.

His right hand was encased in a mitten though it was a hot day. I asked him about it and he pulled off the mitten and showed a white, bloodless hand that he said felt like he was holding ice all the time, though to others it felt warm. The whole time he was talking, I was thinking I must touch that hand and pray.

Suddenly he thrust his hand out and said for me to feel it. I took his warm hand in both of mine and asked him if he had prayed to the Lord about this. He jumped back two feet and jerked his hand out of mine. He said he thought the Lord had sent him the bad hand to keep him from pulling a gun on somebody. I asked if he had shot anyone and he said yes—during the war.

So here was the reason for the bloodless hand—his 40-year guilt from shooting someone in war is still unresolved. We continued to talk and parted in great good humor. I have since prayed for his hand and him also. I hope my concern for him showed a little of Jesus' love. Surely the Lord arranged this meeting. I remembered the Lord had told me to be a witness for him to all I come in contact with.

April 17, 1986—

So much has happened since we returned from Texas. Dad fell and broke his hip. The call about him came at 6:45 A.M. yesterday. He is suffering mightily with the pain but they cannot schedule surgery until his heart and vital signs improve. They also cannot give him pain-killing drugs which depress the heart, so his pain is almost unbearable. Seeing him suffer so is torturing us. We are praying for him and I am trying to teach him to pray. Somehow, he blames us for the fall and the pain. He won't speak to us, but I am trying to work with him with patience, love and gentleness as the Lord said a few days ago. I told him to give Jesus the pain, that Jesus bore all our pains on the cross and he would take the pain away. I believe Jesus did, for Dad doesn't seem to hurt so much now.

April 19, 1986—

Sitting in silence by Dad's bedside has given me time to think. I have been struggling with meanings and purposes of life. True, I love life and have much joy and happiness in all I do. However, it has taken almost 60 years to achieve this state, plus many teachers and preachers, many examples by people I admire, many books and lectures and much suffering and pain on my own part and the part of others in my behalf.

The puzzling part is that God has to start over with every person. No one can learn for the next generation. We can teach, but we cannot learn for them. Great religious revivals and achievements in one generation mean nothing to the next generation. All the suffering and work and study by one does not automatically boost another. Great teachers exhaust themselves in a single generation. But more great teachers seem to appear to take their places. This is God's plan.

April 21, 1986 –

Howard and I went to the altar last night and knelt as a proxy for Dad and received anointing and prayers of all the worshippers. It was a very moving experience. The remainder of the night, I felt the Spirit. There were times when the warmth of the Holy Spirit covered me and once I felt what seemed to be a wave of Spirit move through my body. I prayed that Dad would have the peace of the Spirit too. This morning I feel healed from the head cold that was starting.

During the night I woke singing, "Thou hast made death glorious and triumphant; for through its portals we enter into the presence of the living God;" and "Thine be the glory, risen conquering Son; endless is the victory thou over death hast won." The Lord is preparing us for Dad's death and has directed me to the love chapter in 1 Corinthians 13 and the resurrection passages of 15:22 & 57: *For as all die in Adam, so all will be made alive in Christ. ... But thanks be to God, who gives us the victory through our Lord Jesus Christ.*

April 24, 1986 –

Today Dad is beginning to eat after refusing food, liquid and speech to anyone for the two days following surgery. He still will not speak to us. We spent two days sitting by his bedside after surgery plus the week before surgery. Somehow he blames us for who knows what?

April 26, 1986 —

Yesterday I awoke to hear a voice saying, "*Last chance!*" It was definite and unmistakable. I went to the creek to walk the woods' trail and think. Surely the Lord is telling me to talk with Dad about his status with Jesus. He has been a Christian in name for a long time, but what is the real status of his soul? I hurried to the hospital and told Dad that the Lord had sent me and that the Lord would sometime send for him because he wanted Dad to live with him, but the Lord couldn't have anger in his house so Dad would have to give up his longstanding anger at his father and also whatever he was mad at us about. He nodded acknowledgement but said nothing. I tried to get him to say he accepted Jesus as Savior, but he wouldn't say it aloud. He did grip my hand tightly the whole time so I felt no rejection of what I had been saying. I prayed for him, asking forgiveness for him and felt the Lord's approval of my efforts. I knew the Lord could see into Dad's heart.

April 29, 1986 —

The Lord told me to go quickly to Dad and tell him we love him and the Lord loves him. Three times today I repeated that message and recounted all the nice things he has done in his life. I told him he could go to the nursing home Friday.

May 8, 1986 —

Dad is back in the nursing home but very sick. I told him I thought the Lord may be sending for him and that he should not be afraid for he would see his loved ones who have gone on before him. I told him he would live with the Lord and then asked him if he wanted that and if he took Jesus as his Savior, and he said, *"Yes!" Praise God!*

May 12, 1986—

At Communion last night, I concentrated on the meaning of the elements and praised God. My body became very warm at the altar rail and the warmth continued back in my seat.

Sunday, we sat at Dad's bedside and talked to him softly and gently, speaking of the things he did and the things we did together. He responded warmly. Today he is angry again at something unknown. This vacillating mood is hard to cope with. The Lord sent the hymn "Blessed Assurance" to comfort us.

May 15, 1986—

At last, Dad responded to us in warmth last evening. I told him we loved him. Then I said we were sorry we had not told him that more often. He said, "Oh, you did all right." He was very near death yesterday. Today he looks better.

The Lord gave us a brief respite from the stress of Dad's dying. We drove a few miles to a park where warblers feed while migrating and walked several wooded trails while praying. The Lord rewarded us by presenting a magnolia warbler and a Blackburnian warbler in plain view. On the way back, the Lord sent the hymn, "Because he lives, I can face tomorrow." It comforted me all day. God has also been saying, "Little David, play on your harp," to encourage me to read Psalms.

May 23, 1986—

Dad died last night. I cried hard when I saw his still white face, and so did Howard. It is such an awesome sight to see what was once moving features become so unresponsive and still. I believe and have strong faith in the hereafter, but just because it is so strange, I asked the Lord for confirmation.

It came—*double!* This morning I found myself singing, "Give my regards to Broadway, *remember* me to Herald Square; *tell all the gang* at 42nd Street that *I will soon be there* ... " I sang this half the morning before I realized the Lord was sending it because of Dad—that *Dad* is having a reunion with all the folks who have gone before, just as I told him.

May 24, 1986 —

Another confirmation came today. I opened the book of Psalms, as the Lord suggested last week, and it opened on Psalm 84:1, *How lovely is your dwelling place, O Lord of hosts!* So Dad is presently finding how lovely it is in heaven. O Lord, how can anyone doubt you—who knows even our thoughts before we think them, who leads us gently by the hand when we only start to lift a finger and who guards us from every danger except our own willful sinning?

It seems as though the only way the Lord has of enforcing his perfection through us is by withholding his Spirit when we insist on our own sinful way. The emptiness of life without his Spirit is so painful; it quickly brings us to the realization of where we have sinned. David wrote about this in Psalm 51.

I became aware of a spiritual event around nine Thursday evening—when Dad was dying. Earlier I had been depressed, wanting to cry. I couldn't explain it. The nursing staff called at 9:45 P.M. and said Dad had died. But his spirit passed at around nine, or possibly seven minutes sooner. Two weeks ago I had a vision of a clock set at seven minutes to nine. At that time I didn't know how to interpret it. The Lord knows not only the past, but also the future—and exactly when we are going to die.

This is one of life's great mysteries. We have free will, but the Lord knows what we will choose and where it will take us.

Today I feel as though I were coming out of a long deep sleep or illness. The night of Dad's death, we lay awake all night because of the shot of adrenaline our bodies received. There were white vapors of angels present much of the night. I spoke to them aloud but received no answer. Perhaps I was too upset to hear a spiritual voice.

May 25, 1986 —

Monday we will fly to Ohio to bury Dad in the family plot. His body has already been shipped. In the meantime, this being Sunday, we went to church as usual. Howard broke down a few times, but we were sustained by a church full of concerned friends. At the evening service, Howard and I were called up to kneel at the altar and the congregation laid hands on us and prayed for our safe journey and our well being and peace. It was a wonderful experience. Afterward, someone had brought cake, so we were honored in the parlor with a reception. What absolute joy at our friends' presence and love.

June 7, 1986 —

Everything went well at the funeral and burial. We felt at peace. The countryside was so beautiful; it was an ideal time to be in Ohio.

After the formalities were over, we went to Mohican State Park and walked the trails Dad used to walk with Howard when he was little. The warblers were singing, and the fields were abundantly painted with wild flowers. In the evening, there was a grand reunion of the two estranged sides of the family, which was a great joy to all. Everyone was so kind to us.

June 8, 1986 —

I wrote Meg, my friend in Vancouver, and witnessed to her of my faith and the power of the Spirit I have been experiencing. I told her I love her and God loves her and I am declaring her to be a part of my family so we can go together to live with the Lord. She replied in love, but did not accept my testimony.

Yesterday I failed in discipleship. I lunched with two old friends and participated with them in trivial unimportant gossip, of a sort. I failed to speak up for Christ in places it was needed—in general, failed to live up to Christ in me. So last night the Spirit did not come. Lord, help me to remember who I am in every situation. The Spirit returned rapidly after I asked forgiveness. Thank you, Jesus. I feel like Paul, doing what I don't want to do and refraining from doing things I know to do. Romans 7:15.

June 11, 1986 —

I hummed an unknown tune all day. Finally, I called our choir director and asked what hymn it was. He said, "Sing Praise to God Who Reigns Above."

The words of the third stanza kept ringing in my ear even before I remembered the name of the hymn: "The Lord is never far away, but through all griefs distressing, an ever-present help and stay, our peace and joy and blessing; as with a mother's tender hand, he leads his own, his chosen band, to God all praise and glory."

June 12, 1986 —

Yesterday in the mall, I spoke to a young man, a high school graduate. He was cleaning nearby and something told me to talk to him. He began telling me of an incident when he was eight and cut off his finger with an axe. He ran home with the finger barely hanging by a small bit of flesh. His mother stuck it back together, bound it with tape and hurried him to the church where the congregation quickly gathered to pray for him. The next day, he took off the tape and the finger had reknit completely, including bone.

What tremendous faith of the boy, his mother and the congregation! This incident made such an impression on him that he has decided to become a minister. I wished him God's blessings in his future and we parted. [I never saw him again.]

June 17, 1986 –

Miriam said the Lord gave her a Biblical name. This morning, I asked the Lord if he had a name for me and as soon as I started formulating the question in my mind, the answer came, "Hannah." I feel so honored, because Hannah was a great example of faith and dogged determination and perseverance— also, she was a poet. Hannah means grace.

June 25, 1986 –

I visited my sister Betty for a few days. She told of seeing a vision of a beautiful young woman with blond hair, blue eyes and a smiling face. When she blinked, the vision was gone. I told her it must have been an angel. Driving home later, I hummed a tune all afternoon and when I looked it up, it was, "Angels From the Realm of Glory." Confirmation!

June 27, 1986 –

This morning I woke to hear the Lord say, "July 14, 15 and 16." I asked who this was for, and the answer was, "You." The voice was a deep male voice and the tone was joyful. The Lord has been sending the song, "Let the lower lights be burning;

send a gleam across the waves; some poor fainting struggling seaman, you may rescue, you may save." I am to write my unbelieving friends and tell them about him. Also, I must tell my brother-in-law to use the expression, "God bless," instead of damning everything. That is the reason all his projects turn to ashes in his hands. He asks God to condemn it and God does.

June 28, 1986 —

Again this morning I awakened to a voice calling my name. It was an out-loud deep bass voice.

I drove to the country to pick blackberries and knew the Lord was with me so no snakes, ticks or chiggers would come near. On the way home, a huge pillar of clouds appeared on the horizon directly ahead. They glowed in the late evening sun—pink and white and gleaming. I thought about Moses who followed the clouds by day and fire by night across the desert. I praised God and thanked him for leading me so carefully also.

July 8, 1986 —

We are at Sand Dunes National Monument Campground in Colorado. It is cool, cloudy and a little rainy but so beautiful. I have spent much of the travel time singing hymns out of a Baptist hymn book, just purchased. The Lord has certainly been with us so far and has placed love and kindness in every potentially stressful situation.

I have a feeling the Lord is preparing something very special for me soon. Lord, help me to be faithful—and cleanse me with your sacrificial blood that I may be holy. The blood symbol that I have avoided because it seemed unpleasant has begun to take on new meaning. The blood that ran out of my ear the day James was so angry at me in Sunday school and spoke so harshly has given me a lot to think about. Blood bathes every cell in a living body, nourishes it, oxygenates it, brings it the protection of white blood cells, the instructions of enzymes and the removal of wastes. So when we are symbolically bathed in the blood of Christ, we are nourished, instructed, protected, cleansed and cradled, so to speak. What fantastic symbolism!

July 9, 1986 —

Prayer was very good last night. At one point I felt the Holy Spirit embracing and holding me. It is an all-over warm, tingly and joyful feeling. King David felt this way too, according to Psalm 139:9-10, *If I take the wings of morning and settle at the farthest limits of the sea, even there your hand shall lead me, and* **your right hand shall hold me fast.**

A trail crossed the mountain beside the sand dunes. From the trail, we could view the magnificent pile of sand that measures 50 square miles and rises 800 feet above the valley. Our view went for miles and miles—almost to the town of Alamosa. Behind us, the Sangre De Cristo Mountain Range guards the valley from the east, having presented a formidable challenge to pioneers.

The prickly pear cactus beside the trail was in full bloom, sporting pale lemon-yellow blossoms for its days of glory. Western bluebirds, Cassin's finches and solitary vireos flitted nearby and we could hear the raucous calls of pinon jays and Clark's nutcrackers on the mountain behind us. Then, in a flash, anger broke out over a minor disagreement and the magic was gone.

As we were walking back to camp, a song came into my head. It was "Lord Speak to Me That I May Speak" whose words are: "Lord, speak to me that I may speak in living echoes of thy tone, as thou has sought, so let me seek thy erring children, lost and lone. O, teach me, Lord, that I may teach the precious things thou dost impart. And wing my words, that they may reach the hidden depths of many a heart." Thank you, Lord, for this message.

July 10, 1986 –

Two families of strangers made my prayer list today. One family loaded their car to leave but couldn't get it started. I walked up to the driver's side and asked him if they had prayed for the car to start. He looked perplexed and said, "No."

I said, "Well, take hold of your wife's hand, and she should hold the children's hands and we will pray for the Lord to start your car." He looked as though he were unable to think of any way to get rid of this woman except to do as she said, so he did reach for his wife's hand. I took his hand and simply asked the Lord to fix the car. Then I dropped his hand and walked away quickly. He pressed the starter a few more times, and it caught. I thanked God. This cannot fail to draw the family's attention to higher possibilities.

The second family camped next to us and constant yelling, bickering and harsh sounds issued forth from their direction. Silently, I exorcised evil away from them in Jesus' name and invited in the Holy Spirit. Shortly afterward, I heard laughter and good humor next door. I continued to pray for them as long as we were there. At that point, the Lord sent a hymn, "Take Time to be Holy" – "Speak oft with thy Lord; abide in him always and feed on his word; *make friends of God's children, help them who are weak;* forgetting in nothing, his blessing to seek."

July 13, 1986 –

Sunday we attended a United Methodist church in Alamosa.

The minister was on vacation so an older lay person presided— who did not look well. A woman in the next pew mentioned his name and said he had liver cancer. His sermon was on peace and he reviewed his life work which was devoted to peace. I reached for the pew Bible at the Lord's instruction, and it opened to Isaiah 52:7, *How beautiful upon the mountains are the feet of the messenger who announces peace, who brings good news, who announces salvation, who says to Zion, "Your God reigns."*

I knew immediately it was a message for him, and I was supposed to give it to him and also to pray for him. As we went out among the crowd, I managed to tell him the Lord had sent me to pray for him and I had done so. That evening I wrote a letter and told him the Lord loved him very much and had given me the Isaiah scriptural message to deliver to him. I also said I was praying for him and that my church would pray for him as well. [A year later, we stopped to worship with that church family again. The old lay minister was not in sight, so I asked a parishioner about him. "Oh," she said, "Mr. Farley is on a tour to South America. He is doing fine." Praise God!]

July 14, 1986—

Today the camper stalled on Wolf Creek Pass. The engine overheated and would not start. I began praying and kept it up for possibly a half hour. Then, I said, "Lord, where are you?"

He said, "Calm down, I am sending help." At that moment, a woman highway worker drove up, stuck her head in the camper window and told Howard to remove the air filter and it would start. He did, and it did, and we drove the rest of the mountain road to the campground without the filter. Was she an angel? This was the first of the series of dates the Lord announced to me a few days ago.

July 15, 1986—

Today I was carrying a bucket of water a long distance, and it was getting heavy. All at once, a little girl appeared and asked if she could carry it. She did briefly; then we both shared the handle.

As we walked, I began to talk to her about the Lord and she said she was a Christian. Her little brother and his dog were with her. At the time, I wondered if she were an angel. Their tent camp was near ours and she said her parents had gone fishing. She went into the tent and I never saw her or any of the family including the dog again, even though we were there two more days. Very strange!

July 16, 1986—

The only unusual circumstance today was seeing a fat lady running past our campground. We were walking on the gravel road when this lady came puffing along. She was dressed in shorts and a short sleeved blouse. The mosquitoes were viciously attacking her so I intercepted her and insisted on spraying her bare limbs with an insect repellant we had with us. She thanked us profusely and ran on. Perhaps the Lord sent an angel in trouble to see if we would help her.

July 19, 1986—

Tonight I met a family from Muskogee, Oklahoma who are moving to Albuquerque because of the wife's health. I saw them sitting on a picnic bench so I stopped to talk. When they spoke of her illness, I asked if they believed in faith healing, and they said, "Yes, indeed!" So we all held hands and prayed for the Holy Spirit to bring healing to her and to help the family with their move. I'm sure the Lord was responsible for this meeting.

July 24, 1986 —

We are at Rustler Park, Arizona, in the Chiricahua Mountains. The climb to this 9,000-foot-elevation park was long, rough and narrow. Many times I became frightened at the steepness and rough road. I prayed continually and the Lord helped us make it without problems.

We explored mountain trails where we could observe the desert on both sides of a saddle between mountains. The view is spectacular; I never seem to tire of it. The Lord encouraged me to make the last quarter-mile climb to a fire tower perched on top of a mountain ridge. The view was stunning and I took many pictures. With myriad shades of blue-gray, the Lord painted layer after layer of mountains in the distance. It rained lightly on the way back but I didn't get cold.

Today I talked to a woman whose husband is an atheist. She said their children were converted to Christianity by her baby-sitter while she worked and the children all attend church now. The son wants to be a minister and she is upset because the father and son can no longer communicate. She hates the baby-sitter in an unhealthy manner. I asked if she believed in God and she said yes, so I recommended she ask God every day to take away her anger or it would kill her—besides her anger wouldn't harm the sitter at all. She didn't seem to take offense at this conversation.

July 25, 1986 —

The Lord sent a song early this morning, When I looked it up, it turned out to be, "Thou, My Everlasting Portion" — "More than friend or life to me, all along my pilgrim journey; Savior, let me walk with thee. Close to thee. ... *All along my pilgrim journey; Savior, let me walk with thee.*"

July 26, 1986—

The Lord told me to walk the mountain paths alone this afternoon. I found a place where I could see the distant mountains and deserts and sat there on a log, praying and singing and having a joyful, glorious time. At supper, the words of the fourth verse of the hymn, "I Love Thy Kingdom, Lord," came to me. "Beyond my highest joy, I prize her heavenly ways, *her sweet communion,* solemn vows, her hymns of love and praise."

August 5, 1986—

For the last two days we have driven in desert heat—first northwest of Tucson where the temperature must have been 115° and then through the Mojave Desert of California where at times the terrain looked like the backside of the moon— great mountains of bare rocks. The merciless sun kept getting stronger and hotter. Yesterday rain came in late afternoon and its cooling effect helped us get through the day until we camped at Kingman, Arizona. Our problem was overheating the camper's engine when the air conditioner was on, so some of the time we had to shut down the air conditioner and suffer from the heat.

Safely camped near Bakersfield, I praised God and opened the Bible at random: Psalms 107:4-8, *Some wandered in desert wastes, finding no way to an inhabited town; hungry and thirsty, their soul fainted within them. Then they cried to the Lord in their trouble, and he delivered them from their distress; he led them by a straight way. ... Let them thank the Lord for his steadfast love, for his wonderful works to humankind.*

August 16, 1986—

We are camped in the Olympic National Park in Hoh Valley, a rain forest 30 miles from the Pacific Ocean. We are in the camper and Ann and Clyde, who are with us, have erected a tent. The best day so far was yesterday when we visited Cape Flattery. The cape consists of a high cliff overlooking the ocean on three sides. Great blue waves were constantly crashing into the cliffs and in spite of the violence of the moving water, many seabirds were visible.

This rain forest is luxuriant with all shades of green leaves, mosses, ferns and lichens. I hiked alone yesterday for two hours, talking to everyone along the trail. How lovely are all corners of God's world! It is amazing that everyplace we go to camp, even though crowded, there is always one space left for us. When Ann and Clyde were with us, we entered a camp-ground that was full, except for *two* spaces side by side. They commented on the luck, but I knew who had arranged that.

September 3, 1986 –

We are home again. Yesterday I felt called to the chapel to pray. While kneeling at the altar, I heard the chapel door open and footsteps come down the aisle. I turned to see a tearful woman approaching the altar. As I spoke to her, she started weeping profusely. She said she was ill and afraid. I talked to her and prayed for her. Pastor Charlie came in so I turned her over to him for further counseling and left. Surely the Lord arranged for both of us to be there at that time to help her.

September 11, 1986 –

Yesterday I heard Dr. James Kennedy's say on his radio pro-gram we should not ask the Lord to make every decision for us. If we are in the word and the word in us, we will naturally make godly decisions and should proceed in a loving, peaceful direction with our lives unless we receive a red inner light.

He illustrated it by telling the story of a missionary traveling on foot through the jungles of western Africa following a guide who was moving quite fast along trails and occasionally off the beaten track. At one place, he paused for rest and expressed his alarm over the density of the jungle and the absence of roads, "Is there a map showing these trails that would give one assurance of not becoming lost in the jungle?" The guide replied, "Papa John, I am the map, I am the trail." That is the way we are supposed to work with Jesus—our map and our trail. God's indwelling Spirit leads us in the right direction.

The Lord has been sending a hymn for several nights which expresses in song this same lesson about the missionary and the guide: "Be Thou My Vision" – "O Lord of my heart, naught be all else to me, save that thou art: thou my best thought, by day or by night, waking or sleeping, thy presence my light. *Be thou my wisdom, and thou my true word;* I ever with thee and thou with me, Lord. ... Riches I heed not, or man's empty praise, thou mine inheritance, now and always; *thou and thou only, first in my heart,* ... my treasure thou art."

October 8, 1986–

The terrible flood of 1986 missed our house by two feet. The Lord had sent messages by hymn for several days to be strong and brave. The forecast was for bad flooding and every Scripture I opened mentioned water. On Friday, I awakened at four with a terrible dread in my stomach. I prayed for a while and was still wakeful though tired. So I said, "Lord, send an angel to talk to me, because I can't sleep." Immediately, I slept.

By daylight we wakened to another gray foreboding day, ate breakfast, then I drove to the church chapel to pray. Light poured in the stained glass windows covering me like a protective net and I felt the warmth of the Holy Spirit filling my body. I experienced no more anxiety the entire weekend of flooding. During prayer, I heard someone tell me to call Cindy. Arriving home, I found that Cindy was calling for me. I told her we could use help. She and Roger came immediately to help us put up furniture and clean out bottom drawers. We all stood in the middle of the living room and asked God to send angels around our house to protect it. Cindy is a powerful prayer partner and her strong faith helped us sustain ours.

We carried clothing and valuables to the camper, drained the toilet and stuffed rags in it to protect against sewer back-up. Then the long vigil began. All day Friday, and all that night without taking our clothes off and all the next day, we sat listening to radio reports, watching the flood from our end of town. Occasionally, we walked to the back of the block where boats were carrying people away from houses already flooded. People who have lived here 50 years felt safe, because waters have never been this high in recorded history. The faces of those being carried away witnessed to the trauma of a period they will never forget. I hurt with them.

Saturday the water crept across the block, rose on Oak Street behind us and Cedar Street in front of us. When it entered the southwest corner of our yard Saturday evening, we decided the time had come to go. We drove away in the camper and parked in the church parking lot overnight. Our next-door neighbor to the south sent his family to a friend's house, but he would wait and watch through the night, he said.

The next morning we drove home to find our house high and dry. The neighbor who remained said his ground-level playroom had flooded but the water had been stayed two linear feet from our foundation. Praise God! However, he didn't understand why his house had flooded and ours hadn't since there isn't that much difference in elevation between the two.

This morning I woke up singing the hymn, "He Hideth My Soul" – "A wonderful Savior is Jesus my Lord, a wonderful Savior to me; he hideth my soul in the cleft of the rock where rivers of pleasure I see. He hideth my soul in the cleft of the rock that shadows a dry, thirsty land; *he hideth my life in the depths of his love, and covers me there with his hand."*

October 20, 1986 –

I kept singing "He Hideth My Soul in the Cleft of the Rock" until I wearied so I asked the Lord for something else. He said I hadn't absorbed that yet; nevertheless he did send "His Eye is on the Sparrow and I Know He Watcheth Me."

The lesson for Sunday school this morning was the building of the ark of the covenant and the Tabernacle in Exodus 27-32. There were detailed instructions on how to build it and they were not to vary from these instructions. God is perfection and can only be approached in *perfection—or* because of *Jesus,* by acceptance of our being forgiven. This is why we lean on Jesus.

October 30, 1986 –

I have been wondering about Satan. How can one tell if the message that comes at night is from God or Satan since Satan has the power to imitate God? Immediately the second verse of the hymn "Onward Christian Soldiers" came to me. *"At the sign of triumph, Satan's host doth flee;* On then, Christian soldiers, on to victory! *Hell's foundations quiver at the shout of praise;* brothers, lift your voices, loud your anthems raise!" So praise is what drives Satan away—praise of Jesus and of God!

December 5, 1986 –

I heard a radio program today where a woman emphasized

the need to praise the Lord for everything, including tragedies. She and her daughter had been trapped in a terrible fire and both were severely injured. She learned thro ugh this tragedy to trust in the Lord, leaning on God when all other hope is gone, and to praise the Lord even for bad things. Even David says in Psalms 51:8, *Let me hear joy and gladness; let the bones that you have crushed rejoice.*

My friend Jenny said praising the Lord for frustrations and thorns in the flesh brings unspeakable joy. It brings our mundane events into perspective and shrinks them to unimportance when they are compared with spending an eternity with Jesus.

December 18, 1986 —

In a dream I saw my sister disappear by passing through a wall! It frightened me badly, reminding me of the date of December 29 that was given two weeks ago in the middle of the night by an unknown voice. What is going on? If this is of the Lord, he will confirm it—which I asked for the next night, but *it did not come!* Praise God! Somehow I must learn God's voice so Satan cannot confuse me. We invited my sister and her husband for a visit on December 22 and 23. I will see her and pray for her at close hand.

December 21, 1986 —

Three men have been horribly burned in a construction fire in town. Two have such extensive burns they may not survive. Within an hour word came over the prayer chain and we all engaged in unceasing prayer for them and for the custodian who pulled them out of the explosion and received severe burns on his hands. After several days they are all still alive. The custodian reported his burning hands stopped hurting in the night and healed rapidly. [All the injured men recovered and eventually returned to work. Prayer does make a difference.]

December 24, 1986 —

We had a joyous visit with my sister and her husband during the past two days. I prayed for her and know she will be all right. During prayer tonight, I saw purple—the Lord's color—a deep, rich, velvety hue. [Little did I know at that time that this simple vision of a beautiful color was the beginning of a series of magnificent visions to occur soon.]

January 5, 1987 —

We are at Longview, Texas, heading for the Gulf Coast and then to Florida. Alone in the Toyota, I listened to Frances McNutt's tapes on healing. I am preoccupied with Jesus' healing ministry because of a discussion in the Sunday school. David Cook said Jesus fled from healing because he did not come primarily to heal, but to teach. I leaped out of my seat and said Jesus came declaring the Kingdom of God to be at hand and that the Kingdom consists of physical, mental, emotional and spiritual healing. They are what salvation is. Afterward a few people smiled broadly at me and wished us well on our trip.

January 11, 1987 —

I awakened yesterday with a dream of death of a dear one. This is the second such frightening dream. I don't know who is sending these dreams because I called and the person is well. It seems the closer we approach to Christ and doing his will, the stronger the attacks of the Evil One. As 1 Peter 5:8 says, *Discipline yourselves, keep alert. Like a roaring lion your adversary the devil prowls around, looking for someone to devour.*

Tonight the Lord sent us to a little Methodist church at

Wakulla, Florida. It was glorious—singing, Bible study, healing service and prayer. The people who attend are like a family and show much love for each other and for us. The Lord had sent us there. The minister, Howard Almand, has retired twice before and is now preaching again. He spoke from the heart, in a soft emotional voice, of his faith. When the song leader asked for a request and I thought of the hymn, "He Lives." I opened the hymnal directly to it first thing. The Lord is so good, confirming his presence continually. What a splendid little church! We will come back through here on our way home.

January 12, 1987–

Today I played New Testament tapes while driving. I detected an element of rejection of this life in the gospels—an emphasis on heaven and the coming age. The explanation is that humankind sold out to Satan—who has control of this world and has perverted many of the good things of God.

This musing was rapidly answered by the Lord. While I prepared supper, he sent a verse of "A Charge to Keep I Have" – "a God to glorify, who gave his Son my soul to save and fit it for the sky. *To serve the present age, my calling to fulfill. O may it all my powers engage to do my master's will.* Arm me with jealous care, as in thy sight to live; and O thy servant, Lord, prepare a strict account to give." My calling then is to live in this present age, no matter how perverted it is by Satan.

January 15, 1987–

We met Zacchaeus yesterday. He was a small man, obviously Jewish, named Sam. He and his wife camped near us at Juniper Springs. He talked constantly, was impulsive, a little pushy, and laughed a lot. Thin and short-legged, he walked quickly and I could see him climbing a tree—taking Jesus home with him and resolving to sell his goods and give half to the poor.

January 20, 1987—

A new attitude has taken over my Bible study preparations. I study and fill blanks as though the Lord were teacher. I try to understand and not just skip difficult parts. Working on the Word of God, even Old Testament, is very exciting.

January 21, 1987—

Since Nancy said God's color is purple—and she sees that color at times when her eyes are closed and God is very near— I have seen it several times. It is a rich dark purple—overpowering! It has intensity as if a bright light were shining through an unbelievably rich, stained glass window.

January 28, 1987—

For the past week I have been as sick as I can remember being for several years. We are at Titusville awaiting my recovery before going on to Ft. Myers. The Lord has been with us and arranged for me to have medicine. We were comforted and helped in many ways. I listened to the radio and Bible tapes— and prayed continuously. The Lord has sent his purple light often. One day he sent a brilliant emerald-green light. I wonder what that means? One morning God awakened me with the message, "You will be a witness for me to *men and angels.*"

January 30, 1987—

I have recovered sufficiently for travel, so we drove on to Ft. Myers where we secured a camping place only because someone had just checked out unexpectedly. Life is becoming easier. Today the sky was the most beautiful turquoise-blue—a purity beyond belief. Thank you, Father. He is also sending a song with the phrase, "I can make a perfect heart."

February 3, 1987—

Sunday was Communion day at church. At the time, I visualized the Lord Jesus himself handing me the bread and saying, "This is my body." Later when I began to wonder if my illness were really over, he reminded me of this—that he had given himself to me personally and I would be completely healed. I have not doubted since.

I have resolved to pray and walk every morning to start the day. I must take more time to study and meditate. This will invite the joy which brings healing and everything else I need. For the first time on this trip, I don't hurt someplace or feel sick. It has been a rough winter.

February 19, 1987—

We are camped at the Goldcoaster Campground in Florida City near Homestead. It is quiet, and we have had lots of rest. I felt once today that the Lord Jesus himself was with us and I could see his smile and nod as he showed us the beautiful scenes of the Florida Keys and enjoyed them with us. Also, *I sensed that there is some tremendous experience to come to me in this life. I have felt this at times for several years.*

An opportunity came to witness to two people at this campground. One had a neck brace who said she had severe arthritis. I asked her if she had tried prayer. She said no, that she had been in a hospital for a year with the illness and abruptly turned away from me.

The second was a man we saw watching pelicans beg from fishermen who would occasionally toss them a small fish. He turned to me and said, "These pelicans know what to eat to prolong their lives, but what do you suppose people should eat to live the maximum length of time?"

I said, "Why do you want to prolong it?"

"Well, I certainly don't want to die soon. I don't know what is beyond."

"I do."

"What's that?"

"Heaven!"

"Do you really believe that?"

"I'm certain of it," I said. "It will be so glorious that this life will pale in comparison. Trust in the Lord and you don't have to fear anything."

I don't remember anymore of the conversation. He drifted away and so did we. [Three years later, I wonder why I didn't pursue the subject and tell him the story of Jesus and his saving love. At that time I didn't know how, but I do now.] These two people may be the ones to which the Lord was referring when he said I would be a witness for him to men and angels. Perhaps the pelican watcher was an angel.

February 24, 1987—

I had a dream that revived a painful memory. Waking, I grieved the loss of friends and my suffering. Turning on the radio I heard a minister discussing suffering—which is a gift of God and accomplishes five scriptural purposes:

1. Suffering tests our faith: *So that the genuineness of your faith—being more precious than gold that, though perishable, is tested by fire—may be found to result in praise and glory and honor when Jesus Christ is revealed* (1 Pet 1:7).
2. Suffering purifies us for the kingdom: *It was fitting that God, for whom and through whom all things exist, in bringing many children to glory, should make the pioneer of their salvation perfect through sufferings* (Heb 2:10).

3. Suffering preaches the gospel of Christ's suffering: *I want to know Christ and the power of his resurrection and the sharing of his sufferings by becoming like him in his death* (Phil 3:10).

4. Suffering supplies an example to those who are weak: *If we are being afflicted, it is for your consolation and salvation; if we are being consoled, it is for your consolation, which you experience when you patiently endure the same sufferings that we are also suffering* (2 Cor 1:6) and *For to this you have been called, because Christ also suffered for you, leaving you an example, so that you should follow in his steps* (1 Pet 2:21).

5. Suffering helps us look forward to heaven: *But rejoice insofar as you are sharing Christ's sufferings, so that when you may also be glad and shout for joy* (1 Pet 4:13).

It is marvelous that every problem I have is instantly seized by the Lord and the answer comes immediately in whichever way is convenient at the time. What a magnificent God!

February 25, 1987—

The Lord sent us a gift today. What should we find at New Smyrna Beach but northern gannets flying over the surf! How thrilling to find a "life bird" [species we have never seen before] at a place we have been many times. It made the trip back to Titusville worth the effort. The Lord halted a long hike we had started by sending rain so we would be at the beach at the proper time to see the gannets. Praise him!

Also, Howard's hands have stopped trembling—almost. The prayers for him are sprouting. I have stopped exorcising Satan and am simply praising God for every person and situation.

I am convinced that all universes and all worlds and everything that is, living and non-living, feed constantly on God's energy and exist only because of God's continual and intentional input of energy and being into it. If God were for the smallest fraction of a second to withhold his will and energy from something, it would cease to exist.

Last night the Lord sent a wave of warmth that lasted a long time. He knows I need kidney regeneration and promised to send it. Praise him for his mercy. I also believe God sends a shield to protect me from my enemies. Like Paul, I need to forget the past and press on toward the goal of Jesus (Phil 6:13-14).

Today while driving I finished the New Testament tapes. I played Revelation twice because the Lord has been encouraging me to study this for a while. Tonight the Lord sent a hymn, "Where Cross the Crowded Ways of Life" – "where sound the cries of race and clan, above the noise of selfish strife, we hear thy voice, o Son of man. O master from the mountainside, make haste to heal the hearts of pain, among those restless throngs abide, o tread the city's streets again. ... *Till glorious from thy heaven above shall come the city of our God.*"

February 28, 1987–

I heard this story on the radio today. A woman asked a minister if he had children. He said yes so she then asked if he would consider relegating them to hell forever. He said, "Of course not!"

She asked, "Then why do you think God would send any of his children to hell if you wouldn't allow yours to go?"

His answer: "My dear, God's children do live in heaven with him. But the people who go to hell are Satan's children. They have chosen Satan, so they live with him." Wow!

March 2, 1987–

Yesterday we enjoyed another glorious Sunday. Again we attended Wakulla United Methodist and were warmly welcomed by the people—a small congregation of 45—and the minister who delivered a sermon on God's miracles and how miracles are possible here and now. All we have to do is ask, believing, and God will grant them. God can restore people's relationships to each other and to him. Again, the only requirement is to ask.

Reverend Almand and his wife are among the most gracious and loving Christian people we have ever met. He is retiring in June so we may return for a party they will have to honor him.

March 3, 1987–

Recently I have been musing and meditating on the nature of Jesus. He is divine and alive now because he communicates with me, and I know he loves me. But what about his divinity prior to his birth?

This afternoon I took a nap and found myself semi-awake at one time, saying from Paul, *Let the same mind be in you that was in Christ Jesus, who, though he was in the form of God, did not regard equality with God as something to be exploited, but emptied himself, taking the form of a slave, being born in human likeness. And being found in human form, he humbled himself and became obedient to the point of death—even death on a cross. Therefore God also highly exalted him and gave him the name that is above every name, so that at the name of Jesus every knee should bend, in heaven and on earth and under the earth, and every tongue should confess that Jesus Christ is Lord, to the glory of God the Father* (Phil 2:5-11).

So, back flew the answer: Yes, Jesus did exist with God before the world was created. Other Scriptures say the same thing: John 1:1-3; Psalms 110:1; Genesis 1:26.

Later the Lord said, "I want you to be completely and utterly honest." I puzzled over this, wondering when I had been dishonest and could not remember anytime recently. Later I found myself working through the bird field guide counting the species of birds we have seen in the U.S. and Canada during our 25 years of tabulating (572). A few species I struggled with, wondering if we had really seen them. *Then* it came to me that God was telling me in advance to be strictly honest in the count. It is awesome that he anticipates what I am going to do before I do it.

March 6, 1987—

I walked two miles today, praying and talking with God. It was a beautiful, sunshiny, warm day for early March. At one point I was thinking about the kind of faith necessary to move mountains and just how, physically, a mountain could move. Remembering my February 25 entry about God being consciously and purposefully within everything that is or it would cease to exist, I thought that if he would withhold energy from a mountain, it would disappear. Then he could re-insert that mountain energy into the sea, and it would reappear in the sea. I said to myself that one would need to be very holy and perfect to ask for that to happen. The Lord seemed to say, "No, just have the faith." I decided to try it on something simple so would ask in faith for the Lord to remove a mole on my chest.

Later I said, "Lord, if your energy is in everything that is— keeping it going—how can Satan do anything to it?"

He said, "Satan interferes with the natural processes of life."

"Why do you allow it?"

He said, "You choose it."

*That the creation itself will be set free from its **bondage to decay** and will obtain the freedom of the glory of the children of God* (Rom 8:21).

March 9, 1987—

Yesterday afternoon I awakened from a short nap with the message, "Nothing doubting." This must have been God's confirmation of my decision to test his promise to remove mountains if we have the faith. The mountain I chose was the mole on my chest. [Although moles all over my body peeled off during the next few months, the one on my chest never did. Two years later a surgeon removed it. My faith still has a long way to go.] All during the evening church service and Communion I felt God's Spirit heat in my body. This lasted for a long time afterward. Thank you, Father. He asked me recently to call him Father instead of Sir.

March 10, 1987—

We drove to Carthage last night with Roger and Cindy to hear Dr. Bill preach a revival sermon. He delivered an outstanding message on discipleship and told of a woman who gave up her job in a bank rather than carry out dishonest policies her boss assigned her to do.

The Spirit was very present in that church and on the way home. I was so keyed up it was after one before I went to sleep. A little later, I awakened for some reason and it was very quiet. The room and my spirit were much at peace. I asked the Lord to send an angel but nothing happened, so I closed my eyes and said, "If the angel Amersa is here, touch me so I will know it." Nothing.

I almost went back to sleep, but something drew my eyes open again. *A brilliant green light* swept across my eyes from left to right and across my hand, which was holding the covers close to my face. This light grew more and more intense until the whole room was flooded with a brilliant emerald-green light. At the same time, my body tingled all over in a very strange manner I have come to know when the Spirit of the Lord embraces me.

At that point, I became frightened—I don't know why—but I didn't know what to expect next and was afraid of the unknown. As soon as I felt fear, the green light receded and disappeared. I closed my eyes and saw the beautiful, deep velvety purple of God's color briefly, then promptly went to sleep.

This morning, the tune of an old secular song pressed into my consciousness: "If I Had the Wings of an Angel." Then I *knew* the green moving light I saw last night was the wing of an angel. That also explains the green color I saw in Florida last winter when I was so sick. At that time it was also quite vivid and I saw it in the daytime with my *eyes closed.*

Later this morning, the words to a hymn came to me: "The Lord haste the day when my faith shall be sight." How absolutely wonderful! I must pray that the Lord will help me not to fear. No telling what the next step is. Praise the Lord! My joy today is so overwhelming I can hardly wait to tell Miriam.

March 12, 1987–

Last night I had a terrible stomachache—particularly in the lower right abdomen. I lay awake much of the night praying and putting warm hands on the hurting place. No time did I feel the Lord telling me to go to the doctor. Much of the night, I felt Spirit heat healing me. This morning the pain is almost gone. The Lord sent the hymn "Trust and Obey."

March 13, 1987–

Yesterday I was so busy I ignored the vestiges of the pain in my stomach, but while working I continued to think about the Lord from time to time. Almost at once, the hymn came to me with the words, "Where cross the crowded ways of life, where sound the cries of race and clan, above the noise of selfish strife, *we hear thy voice, o Son of Man.*" Even though busy with the day's activities, the voice of the Lord comes through.

Recently I visited Rose [mentioned Jan. 31, 1986 above] who has bone cancer. I took her a *Guidepost* which contained an article on the miraculous healing of a woman with bone cancer. I told her to have faith in Jesus and that death is not the end. She said she did have faith and was better. Praise God!

March 16, 1987—

"Dare to be different" was the word from the Lord this morning. Again, I am having abdominal pain. Hazel prayed for me and with me Sunday night and I felt the heat of the Holy Spirit for a long time.

March 17, 1987—

Private worship was powerful last night. As I read and studied the Word, I glanced from time to time at the copy of the Turin portrait of Jesus nearby.

I turned out the light and prayed with eyes open, half expecting the eyes of Jesus in the painting to light up, but instead, *bright tongues of fire* shot out from around the picture. I was startled and a little frightened. I quickly reached for the light switch, turned it on and regained my composure. I put the picture away and went to bed.

As I became quiet, and my eyes adjusted to the dark, I saw *tongues of fire* around me! I looked at my hands, and the fire was coming from *my hands also*! I was actually seeing the fire of the *Holy Spirit of God* around me in the bedroom. So I laid my hands on my hurting stomach and went to sleep. What wondrous things are happening to me! Praise the Lord!

Perhaps this is what John the Baptist meant as the baptism of fire: *"I baptize you with water for repentance, but one who is more powerful than I is coming after me; I am not worthy to carry his sandals. He will baptize you with the Holy Spirit and fire"* (Mt 3:11). And as the Psalmist puts it: *You makes the winds your messengers, fire and flame your ministers* (104:4).

At the insistence of Miriam and Hazel, I went to the doctor about my abdominal pain. He found nothing but insisted I return for a complete check-up in two weeks. [The later check-up also revealed nothing out of order in my body.]

March 23, 1987–

Miriam said the Lord would give me anything I asked for, so I asked for two things—health and energy to live in order to do his work and hear his voice better. The gift of prophecy is supposed to be the greatest gift. But if I can hear his messages clearly, that is equivalent to prophecy.

Tonight the Bible opened to Isaiah 49:1-3: ... *The Lord called me before I was born, while I was in my mother's womb he named me. He made my mouth like a sharp sword, ... and he said to me, "You are my servant."*

March 26, 1987–

News came that an old acquaintance, Lil Blassingame, is in the hospital and near death; also Henry Bales has incurable pancreatic cancer. After working at home until afternoon, I heard the Lord say, "Go pray for Lil and tell her of me."

I questioned whether Miriam—who knew her better than I did—shouldn't go, but the order seemed clear that I was to go. Still I hesitated so said, "Please send a confirmation." I received three: The command to find the one lost sheep (Mt 18:12); the story of Paul's laying hands on sick Publius to heal him (Acts 28:8); and the charge not to be ashamed of the gospel (Lk 9:26). So I called Miriam to go with me.

A parking place opened on the first level of the hospital parking garage. When we arrived at the room, Lil was alone. Miriam has such a remarkable way with people. She spoke softly and tenderly of love and concern for Lil and told her of a healing the Lord had done at her request on a woman with an unborn breach baby [God righted the baby in the womb]. When she asked if we might pray with her, Lil agreed and Miriam made a gentle prayer of love and trust in Jesus and a request for healing of the Lord for Lil. Lil struggled to keep from crying. We departed satisfied the Lord had heard our prayer.

Strangely, the Lord then told me to go to the shopping mall and talk to the popcorn vendor whom I knew to be a person of faith. In talking, the vendor mentioned his wife had been completely healed of pancreatic cancer by the prayers of doctors at Tulsa's City of Faith Hospital. I knew then that it was meant for me to go to Henry and his wife, Denise, and tell them there is hope for him from the Lord through the City of Faith doctors.

March 27, 1987—

While pondering yesterday's message, I decided to go to the creek this morning to look for blue-gray gnatcatchers—a very early migrant bird. Avoiding the issue for two hours, I hunted vainly for the gnatcatcher. Finally, I said, "Shouldn't I just write Denise a note and tell her?" The problem was that Henry and I had a major contention which resulted in my loss of 30 years of church friendships. He didn't want to see me, and I didn't necessarily want to see him.

The Lord said, "No, go to their door and tell Denise personally." At that moment, a gnatcatcher sounded off in a tree just over my head, the first one of the morning. Confirmation!

After shedding a few tears, I offered up my unforgiveness of Henry on the altar of obedience and watched it burn out. I was now free to accomplished the assignment in the afternoon. A daughter answered the door. Henry was in the hospital and Denise was with him, she said. I told her the whole story and gave her the name of the popcorn man with whom to confirm it. Then I told her to tell Denise and Henry that I love them and the Lord Jesus loves them.

All the way home a hymn tune was running through my mind. It was, "Glorious Things of Thee are Spoken" – "Zion, city of our God; he, whose word cannot be broken, *formed thee for his own abode. On the Rock of Ages founded, what can shake thy sure repose? With salvation's walls surrounded, thou may'st smile at all thy foes. ... Round each habitation hovering, see the cloud and fire appear.*"

Thank you, Father. This is a comforting message to remind me of your grace. This hymn mentions the fire I see at night and is like the fire and cloud of Moses in Exodus 13:21: *The Lord went in front of them in a pillar of cloud by day, to lead them along the way, and in a pillar of fire by night, to give them light.* Also the Holy Spirit fell on the early church in the form of fire, Acts 2:2-3: *And suddenly from heaven there came a sound like the rush of a violent wind, and it filled the entire house where they were sitting. Divided tongues, as of fire, appeared among them, and a tongue rested on each of them.*

A hymn came this splendid day when I was able to do so much without doubting the little voice: "Rejoice, Ye Pure in Heart" – "rejoice, give thanks and sing; your glorious banner wave on high, the cross of Christ your king. Bright youth and snow-crowned age, strong men and maidens fair; raise high your free, exulting song, *God's wondrous praise declare.*"

March 29, 1987 –

I visited Lil both yesterday and today. Yesterday, however, I saw Denise and her daughters at the hospital. Denise grabbed me around the neck and cried. I repeated the story of the City of Faith doctor and urged her to take Henry there as his only chance. She said it was up to Henry. They would listen to the Lord and do as he says.

Today I have thought, Henry has a choice. He can reject this good news from the Lord because it comes through me—and he will die—or he can choose Christ's agent in the City of Faith and live—which is what God told me to tell him. [Henry did not accept the message, but now from his station in heaven, he can rejoice that God turned injury into good for both me and the Kingdom.]

It is tragic how one agent of Satan can contaminate such a large group of people including my friend Henry. Possibly, this is the reason for clusters of the same illness cropping up from time to time in various parts of our country and the world also—or violence that becomes epidemic in places. I am beginning to delve very deep—it almost scares me. But I am covered by the blood of Christ, praise the Lord. Nothing can hurt me.

One of God's dove-tail miracles occurred Sunday when the gospel lesson answered two last sentences of the previous entry. *The 70 returned with joy, saying, "Lord, in your name even the demons submit to us!" He said to them, "I watched Satan fall from heaven like a flash of lightning. See, I have given you authority to tread on snakes and scorpions, and over all the power of the* *enemy; and **nothing will hurt you**"* (Lk 10:17-19).

March 30, 1987–

The Lord confirmed yesterday's message by sending the hymn, "He Leadeth Me" – "O blessed thought! O words with heavenly comfort fraught! *Whate'er I do, where'er I be, still tis God's hand that leadeth me. ...* His faithful follower I would be, for by his hand he leadeth me." I thanked the Lord for guiding me in a most wonderful way. Then I went to bed late after kneeling and thanking God for Jesus. My feet were so cold I lay on my back to straighten the legs and gain better circulation. In the darkened room it appeared that spirits were gathering and swirling around me. They were concentrated directly in front of me. I asked the Lord if angels were here.

He said, "A big party." I asked why. He said it was a celebration. He told me to look at my hands. I shifted my gaze to my hands which were folded together in prayer. They were enclosed in a heavy vapor.

The Lord said, "See, I am covering your hands with mine. *You will have the ability to lay your hands on the sick and pray for them, and they will recover!*" I was almost in shock! But I was wide awake. I prayed and exorcised Satan from the room just in case the spirits were the wrong kind. I also prayed to be covered by the blood of Christ. Nothing changed. Eventually the vapors faded. I asked God for a confirmation and he sent me to the Scriptures. He said *immediately,* so I got up, went to the kitchen and opened the Bible to 1 Corinthians: *And God has appointed in the church first apostles, second prophets, third teachers; then deeds of power, then **gifts of healing,** forms of assistance, forms of leadership, various kinds of tongues* (12:28).

I asked the Lord for whom to pray for healing. He said I

was to choose, but he would help. He said prayer and fasting strengthen the healing spirit.

March 31, 1987 –

Today is our 36th wedding anniversary. The Lord sent a hymn to me just as I awakened: "O Perfect Love" – "all human thought transcending, lowly we kneel in prayer before thy throne. That theirs may be the love that knows no ending whom thou forevermore dost join in one. ... Grant them the joy which brightens earthly sorrow, grant them the peace which calms all earthly strife ..."

April 1, 1987 –

Last night the vapors or Spirits were not there but as I looked at my hands I noticed them glowing. Light actually came from my palms! I praised the Lord and cried a little.

April 6, 1987 –

A confirmation was sent last night of the healing gift from the Lord. This past weekend was a busy one with all the trips to the city sponsoring Miriam at the Emmaus Walk. I talked with Miriam on the way back wondering if the covering on my hands and the words telling me to heal were real or imagined.

So it came again last night. In bed with the lights out, I looked at my hands and after a few minutes, a golden glow began to circle them. It looked as though my hands had a golden aura completely around them. I could see all the way through them—like an X ray—awesome! My hands tingled, then my whole body felt warm and electrified. In the morning the room smelled of ozone—as though an electric current had passed through the room all night.

Today Miriam and I laid hands on an old friend who is

losing her memory. I also went to the hospital, laid hands on two children and prayed for them. The Lord sent an approval of this action when the Bible opened to 1 Timothy 4:14: *Do not neglect the gift that is in you, which was given to you through prophecy with the laying on of hands by the council of elders.*

April 9, 1987–

Last night I was ill—with a cold, sinus infection and cough. In spite of this, the Lord sent the most beautiful colors to cover my hands on the sheet. There were purple, gold and blue lights and an iridescent, creamy white radiance that was so bright it was overpowering. It was as though someone above had a spotlight with color plates shining down on me. However the waves were not even. One drifted in before the last had disappeared and the combinations of gold and green or creamy white and red and blue made *colors I have never seen on earth before.* I honestly believe the Lord is allowing me to see through a crack in heaven! *What wondrous things are happening to me!*

My fog-encircled hand was close to my face so I inhaled deeply wanting to draw the Holy Spirit into the lungs. I must have slept then. The next morning the Lord said he was healing the cold and confirmed it by Scripture. *"Ask, and it will be given you; search, and you will find; knock, and the door will be opened to you"* (Luke 11:9).

April 10, 1987–

Last night as I wrote in this journal, colors played around the pen on the white paper—purple, rose, blue, green and creamy white. When I turned out the light and went to bed, a party was already going on—colors flashed around me, coming toward me, and I could feel the embrace of the Spirit—a strange tingly feeling all over, hot spots in various parts of the body, particularly the lungs where I needed the healing from the chest cold.

There was a halo around my hands and I could almost see through them—*I could even see the bones in my hand! The flesh was translucent!* It was still dark, and in the dark, I felt my face tingle and went to the bathroom mirror, *where I saw the blue light coming from my face!*

Back in bed, I looked toward the window and it became very bright with a light extending on the wall around the window as though the window itself had a halo. The curtains appeared to be moving, disturbed by the wind of the Holy Spirit. Though I tried to make figures out of the wavy lines in the room, I never succeeded.

It is hard to describe the awe I felt during these events. That the Lord of the universe, my Savior and my God, descends to visit, comfort and show me a glimpse of heaven is more than my mind can encompass! The cold stopped in its tracks and did not go to the lungs. Praise him who is and was and is to be!

The Lord sent a hymn this morning, "Living For Jesus" by Thomas Chisholm – "Living for Jesus a life that is true, striving to please him in all that I do, yielding allegiance, glad-hearted and free, this is the pathway of blessing for me. O Jesus Lord and Savior, I give myself to thee, for thou in thine atonement, dids't give thyself for me."

April 11, 1987—

This morning the Lord sent a Scripture of the transfiguration: *Six days later, Jesus took with him Peter and James and his brother John and led them up a high mountain, by themselves. And he was transfigured before them, and his face shone like the sun, and his clothes became dazzling white* (Mt 17:1-2).

April 12, 1987—

The Lord sent another Scripture today to explain the light I have been seeing at night. On awaking, I found myself quoting the prologue to the gospel of John: *In the beginning was the Word, and the Word was with God, and the Word was God. He was in the beginning with God. All things came into being through him, and without him not one thing came into being. What has come into being in him was life, and the life was the light of all people. The light shines in the darkness, and the darkness did not overcome it* (1:1-5).

April 15, 1987—

Today Miriam and I went to see Alberta, an old friend who is deteriorating mentally, and we prayed together. I am also going daily to visit and pray for Delilah, a young woman afflicted with M.S. There is no overt change in her body.

April 16, 1987—

The Lord has given me a task to do at church. I was told to conduct a "Service of Praise" in the sanctuary every day of the year. Its primary purpose is to offer praises to God in behalf of the church as a whole and offer thanksgiving to God for sending his son. Additionally, the lay people are to pray for the ministers and the staff by name, as well as the mission, the congregation—especially those with needs—the unchurched and the unsaved in the city, One person is to go to the church everyday and offer these prayers. It should be easy to organize.

April 17, 1987—

A Communion service was held last evening at the regular Sunday night worship. I felt the presence of the Holy Spirit mightily for my hands were hot during the entire service and it seemed that something special was about to happen. It did. Being very tired when we came home, I went to bed and fell asleep immediately. At three I awakened with a start, heard bells ringing deep within my left ear and watched in wonder as *the room was transformed into a hazy, foggy space with the light varying from yellowish to rosy.* I looked at my hands and they flashed white lines of light and red tongues of fire. I felt my face light up as waves of Spirit embraced me—causing tingly, warm, electric-like shocks to run through my whole body. After a bit, I went to the bathroom and saw my face glowing a blue light with pinpoints of bright light darting out of it. It is hard to describe the awe I felt. This is real Communion with the creator of the universe.

After a while I started asking questions. "Shall I drive to Dallas to lay hands on Gary [my friend's brilliant young son in advanced stages of M.S.] and pray for healing?"

"I will honor that effort," the Lord said.

"Should I tell Rose you heard her prayer and will heal her?"

"Yes!"

"Please send a confirmation."

"Go get your Bible." It opened to John 14:12: *Very truly, I tell you, the one who believes in me will also do the works that I do and, in fact, will do greater works than these, because I am going to the Father. I will do whatever you ask in my name, so that the Father may be glorified in the Son. If in my name you ask me for anything, I will do it.*

"Thank you, Father!"

In the morning I asked the Lord to send a confirmation of these happenings so he sent the hymn, "There's a Song in the Air." Parts of the hymn apply to last night: "*We rejoice in the light, and we echo the song that comes down through the night from the heavenly throng.* Aye! We shout to the lovely evangel they bring, and we greet in his cradle our Savior and King.''

Later, the Lord sent the ''Battle Hymn of the Republic.'' Its fourth verse is pertinent: ''In the beauty of the lilies, Christ was born across the sea *with a glory in his bosom that transfigures you and me;* as he died to make men holy, let us live to make men free while God is marching on.'' What wonderful confirmations the Father sent!

The Lord asked me what gift I would like to receive. I was shocked to my toes by the request, but managed to say that the gift of healing he bestowed was so great I was hesitant to ask for anything more. He said he wanted to give me something I wanted, so I asked for ears to hear him better and for energy to serve him. [This answer did not satisfy the Lord, so he searched my hidden longings and two years later made it possible for us to buy a beautiful house on a hill overlooking a lovely valley.]

April 18, 1987—

Today I told Rose the Lord is healing her and the Lord had told me to tell her he had heard her prayers. Her face was pink and healthy-looking and she received the message with a smile. She said she felt fine and could sleep on her side without pain for the first time in a year—also she had been listening to a 24-hour Christian station and was enjoying it. I told her to praise the Lord often, and she smiled. I shall praise him on her behalf.

April 19, 1987—

It was a glorious Easter Day from the sunrise service on top of the parking garage through the morning worship services and the visits and prayers for the sick with Miriam, and then the evening worship. I had an opportunity to touch several people and pray for them in the midst of the crowds.

Last night the Holy Spirit came to me and touched me several times sending waves of warmth and small electric shocks all through me. Light filled the room except for two places on the wall which were coal black. I couldn't explain those black spots, but ordered out evil in the name of Jesus and the light slowly filled them. Perhaps the wall has been damaged by termites. They are gone now, praise God!

Once I saw rapid movement in the room. When I began to be afraid, the Spirit retreated and faded. I am only slowly being able to handle these supernatural visitations at night. I overcame fear by praising God and there was a partial return of the Spirit. The moment I awakened this morning, I looked toward the window which was filled with bright red flames of the Holy Spirit. The duration of the vision was very brief—everything was normal again in an instant. It was a glorious Easter gift from the Lord!

April 25, 1987–

My sister and I went to visit Marie, a dear old lady dying of lung cancer. We held her hands and prayed for the Lord's healing. She is a woman of faith, so she has hope. She would be counted as one of the little people Jesus loved. Though age had faded her features, she still retained the essence of beauty that won contests when she was young. She showed us pictures of earlier times and basked in our admiring comments.

April 26, 1987–

The colors did not come until morning. It was early daylight when the beautiful colored lights appeared to me, playing on my hands. I lay in bed quietly with eyes open enjoying communion with the creator of the universe.

The Lord sent a passage in Isaiah, *In the year that King*

Uzziah died, I saw the Lord sitting on a throne, high and lofty; and the hem of his robe filled the temple. Seraphs were in attendance above him; each had six wings: with two they covered their faces, and with two they covered their feet, and with two they flew. And one called to another and said: "Holy, holy, holy is the Lord of hosts; the whole earth is full of his glory." The pivots on the thresholds shook at the voices of those who called, and **the house filled with smoke** *(6:1-4).*

The colors and lights I have been seeing this spring are described in Revelation 4:1-3: *After this I looked, and there in heaven a door stood open! And the first voice, which I heard speaking to me like a trumpet, said, "Come up here, and I will show you what must take place after this." At once I was in the spirit, and there in heaven stood a throne, with one seated on the throne! And the one seated there looks like jasper and carnelian, and around the throne is a* **rainbow** *that looks like an* **emerald.**

Another reference to the light of God I found in 1 Peter 2:9: *You are a chosen race, a royal priesthood, a holy nation, God's own people, in order that you may proclaim the mighty acts of* **him who called you out of darkness into his marvelous light.**

April 27, 1987 –

It was quiet at the beginning, but as the night progressed, the "holy" fog floated into the room. Isaiah calls it "smoke" and it seemed to be present all night. Every time I wakened, I saw the foggy bedroom. At times the color of the interior light was yellowish, at times pink. Three times I felt the touch of the Spirit. This morning the Lord sent two hymns: "Silent Night" whose third verse mentions light – "Silent night, holy night, Son of God, *love's pure light, radiant beams from thy holy face,* with the dawn of redeeming grace, Jesus Lord at thy birth."

The second hymn was "Away in a Manger," also verse three: "Be near me, Lord Jesus, I ask thee to stay *close by me forever, and love me, I pray.* Bless all the dear children in thy tender care, and fit us for heaven to live with thee there."

Since the Lord sent a hymn about children, I hurried to the hospital and prayed for three babies I didn't know. The parents and grandparents seemed pleased.

April 29, 1987—

Last night instead of plain colors, I saw a kaleidoscope of every color of the rainbow in circles, squares, stars and long rods—different patterns everywhere. In one place, a rainbow appeared clearly in *a straight line* across the window. Light in the room at night is very dim, consisting of moon and stars plus a street light half block away. What a wondrous experience I am having with the creator of the universe!

A large blob of haze entered the room and reached out to me by way of a thin string of fog and I felt the Spirit's embrace. Perhaps when I become more secure, I can see clearly what is touching me.

May 7, 1987—

The past week was busy, busy. Sandra Miller, an old friend, was here for a day and an evening. She was searching for peace and comfort, and we gave it. I spoke long of my experience with God as she listened.

I continue to visit Rose every week. She, who once was an atheist, grasps my hand when we pray and I risk praying aloud. I tell her that everyday she is alive to say, "Praise the Lord."

She answered, "I do, I do!"

The Lord has placed a cross on my forehead. The long vertical line is from surgery, but the crossbar God placed on it as a reminder that I am his and have the honor of suffering in behalf of the gospel. I feel like telling the world, as Paul did in Galatians 6:17: *From now on, let no one make trouble for me; for I carry the marks of Jesus branded on my body.* It is a wonderfully comforting badge. I rarely see nail prints in my hands anymore.

May 10, 1987–

Tonight Howard and I worshipped by ourselves in the camper at Rock Creek State Park because I didn't want to go to church on Mother's Day. I told the Lord I couldn't handle Mother's Day at church, but he said I could if he helped me with it.

May 11, 1987–

Sandra, who visited us last week, has been on my mind and in my prayers continually since her visit. So this morning, while I was walking in the woods at Rock Creek, the Lord told me to write her telling her what Joab said to King David when he was grieving over his son Absalom.

As I turned at the far end of the mountain trail and started back, my thoughts drifted to various things to include in the proposed letter. The next instant I was back at the head of the trail with no knowledge or remembrance of several mud puddles, gullies and difficult parts of the trail. Did God lift me and place me back at the trailhead? At that very moment, the ranger drove by and offered me a ride back to camp, another mile. The Lord is saying to write the letter *now.*

> Dear Sandra,
>
> I have been thinking and praying about you almost continuously since you were here. The Lord finally told me this morning that if I have your name on my ticket, it is my responsibility to give you this message – the same way Joab

spoke the truth to King David in 2 Samuel 19 when David was grieving over the death of his son Absalom.

He says his ear is not deaf that he cannot hear your cry and his arm is not shortened that he cannot help you. He loves you very much – you are one of his own – and when you weep, he weeps. But, he says, you have shut him out. You have relied on your own programming rather than trust in him. You were not willing to turn your son over to him completely, as Abraham did. God rescued Isaac when Abraham passed the test of faith. But you relied on your own mental programming to hold up your son during his Bar Mitzvah, with only a secondary prayer to your God. And, God says, I am not willing to share your devotion with anyone or anything or any device. That approaches idolatry which has been an anathema to God from the beginning.

The only way he could get your attention, says God, was to let your way fail so you would know not to put your trust in yourself but turn to him.

Through centuries and millennia he has supported his children and carried them over impassable places and through impossible situations because he loved them more than any other people. He says in 2 Chronicles: *If my people who are called by my name humble themselves, pray, seek my face, and turn from their wicked ways, then I will hear from heaven, and will forgive their sin and heal their land* (7:14).

I have given much thought to the meaning of sin. Sin is the inflicting of pain or hurt on oneself, one's neighbor, one's environment – which includes all animals and plants, atmosphere and earth, river and ocean – and, most of all, inflicting hurt to God. Failure to do God's will in any affair is also a sin. The Israelites of old knew this so they laid their sin and guilt on a sacrificial animal and killed it as a substitute for themselves.

Christians believe that God finally sent his Son Jesus to volunteer to be the sacrificial victim for all sin for all time for all the world. The Israelites dedicated the life blood of the animal victim to God, so they did not touch the blood. Christians believe Jesus offered his life blood to them symbolically to partake in his life and his sacrifice in order to be restored to God. All that is required to participate in this ultimate forgiveness is to ask for it from God – privately or publicly, silently or aloud. God hears our thoughts and our heart yearnings.

The Lord says to turn your life around and ask his forgiveness. Seek his face and he will be your God and help you. *Trust in the Lord with all your heart, and do not rely on your own insight. In all your ways acknowledge him, and he will make straight your paths* (Prov 3:5-6).

God says he has written his commandments on your heart. You should review them, read your testament and pray every moment each day, trusting in him only. Then he will lead you and restore you one day at a time until you are in perfect peace and joy overtakes you as it did King David when he danced before the Ark.

Your way leads only to destruction and death but God's way leads to life eternal. I am weeping as I write this because I don't know how you will take it but I must write it. I love you and I know God loves you.

Dottie G.

May 12, 1987–

I asked the Lord for confirmation whether to send the letter and the Bible opened to Luke 15:4, 6-7, *"Which one of you, having a hundred sheep and losing one of them, does not leave the ninety-nine in the wilderness and go after the one that is lost until he finds it? ... And when he comes home, he calls together his friends and neighbors, saying to them, 'Rejoice with me, for I have found my sheep that was lost.' Just so, I tell you, there will be more joy in heaven over one sinner who repents than over ninety-nine righteous persons who need no repentance."*

May 17, 1987–

Miriam, Ruby and I are fasting and praying for Rose. Miriam received a message from the Lord that we should do that because Rose is suffering so much pain. The April 17 message I received from the Lord that he was healing her must mean a spiritual healing. I visited her today and came away in peace because I believe she has come to know the Lord. She mentioned seeing her dead mother, father and brother the other night in a vision and they comforted her and told her it would be all right. She says she is ready to go on—she doesn't want to be so much trouble to Alex and doesn't want anymore suffering. I anointed her with oil, prayed with her and kissed her.

This was my first deliberate fast, and I did pray fervently for the relief of Rose's suffering. Fasting enables the presence of the Holy Spirit to be more easily felt. In the night, I saw the Lord's colors again and every once in a while I detected a faint inner ear sound as though from heaven. Once it was tinkling bells and another time voices.

May 19, 1987—

What a marvelous vision last night. Right after retiring, I looked at my hands and saw darts of bright red around them and thin rays of light coming out of the palms extending halfway across the room. I turned them toward the window to receive God's blessings. In a little while I made out a chair—*a throne*—in the window. In the seat the light was brighter than elsewhere in the room. Once I looked away and blinked and when I looked back a very bright light—intense and piercing in the shape of a cross—emanated from the center of the throne. It was brief—a fraction of a second. On looking opposite the throne I saw a single lighted candle on the wall—for a brief fraction of a second. From time to time I saw bright red points of light—like coals of fire—in the room. I prayerfully covered Howard, myself and the whole house with the blood of Jesus. The visions continued—they were from *God!* [Perhaps the vision can be explained by Proverbs 20:27: *The human spirit is the lamp of the Lord, searching every innermost part.*]

I slept for a time then awakened again to see a pattern of green stones like an oriental rug. While wondering why the Lord was sending such a vision, I began to see the pattern as a throne. So what I was seeing earlier in the evening was *a vision of the throne of God!* The throne of Revelation 4:2-3 was like jasper which is a green opaque stone—exactly like what I saw! This God of ours has so much love and glory, he wants to share it. *What a vision!*

The brightest visions come just before sleep or just after waking. Many visions begin with flames or red flickering light before the other things take shape. These visions are so awesome and unbelievable, I wouldn't credence them if they were not happening to me. I am sober, undrugged, awake, with all my faculties. However I find these same phenomena in the Bible in places where God reveals himself.

This morning, I began to hum a song the Lord sent and found it to be: "O perfect love, all human thought transcending, *lowly we kneel in prayer before thy throne.*"

May 20, 1987—

Last night there were no colors—only light and I was so tired I could scarcely watch. The throne was there in the window and on it was a bright object I couldn't identify. Out of the bright object spewed haze or fog that rose like smoke from a chimney, getting fatter as it went up. Some of it appeared to spill over into the bedroom. I felt so comforted and at peace. This morning the Lord sent the hymn, "In the Cross of Christ I Glory." The third verse describes what I saw: "When the sun of bliss is beaming light and love upon my way; *from the cross the radiance streaming adds new luster to the day.*"

May 22, 1987—

All day long during the journey to Wakulla, Florida, the Lord has been sending hymns that have to do with what I have been thinking and praying about. "Gentle Jesus, Meek and Mild" is one: "Loving Jesus, gentle lamb, in thy gracious hands I am. Make me, Savior, what thou art, live thyself within my heart. I shall then show forth thy praise, serve thee all my happy days; then the world shall always see Christ, the holy Child, in me."

I have been praying the blood of Jesus on all situations and persons who are ill or having problems. The hymnal open to "I Hear Thy Welcome Voice" – "that calls me, Lord, to thee, *for cleansing in thy precious blood that flowed on Calvary.* I am coming, Lord! Coming now to thee; *wash me, cleanse me in the blood that flowed on Calvary.*"

Since I saw the throne of God at home on the window by way of a vision, the Lord has sent several hymns containing the phrase "the throne of God." One of them is "O God, Our Help in Ages Past" – "*Under the shadow of thy throne* thy saints have dwelt secure. Sufficient is thine arm alone, and our defense is sure."

He also sent "He Hideth My Soul" – "*When clothed in his brightness,* transported I rise to meet him in clouds of the sky, his perfect salvation, his wonderful love I'll shout with the millions on high." And then to match my feelings of the day came: "O Could I Speak the Matchless Worth" – "O could I sound the glories forth which in my Savior shine, I'd soar and touch the heavenly strings and vie with Gabriel while he sings in notes almost divine." Daniel 12:3 says *Those who are wise shall shine like the brightness of the sky,* and those who lead many to righteousness, like the stars forever and ever.

May 23, 1987—

We attended the retirement party tonight for Rev. Howard Almand. As expected, it was a surprise to him and he was overwhelmed we had come so far to a party for him. It was a grand celebration with some 75 in attendance. Kent, the little boy with spina bifida for whom I have been praying, is better. I held his head for a long time and prayed.

For some reason, I am beginning to notice a pink glow on everything. White paper appears slightly pink and suddenly the phrase "looking at the world with rose-colored glasses" is taking on a literal meaning. [Three years later, this is still true.]

During the last few days I have experienced waves of euphoria—truly the peace that passes all understanding—making me feel of supreme worth in God's sight with a certainty that God is closer than my arm or leg and helping me every step of the way plus a confidence as my guide and companion, keeper and sustainer. He is a friend who loves me beyond comprehension.

May 24, 1987—

Reverend Howard Almand preached another moving sermon at the Wakulla church. His opening remarks to his "little flock" almost broke everyone up—including himself. He weeps easily. His sermon on the Beatitudes was unforgettable. He said there are three guarantees to Spirit-filled Christians: they will be full of joy; they will never be afraid again; and they will most certainly be persecuted. Amen to that.

We spent a peaceful and quiet night in our camper, parked in the church lot. The only noise we heard was the call of limpkins. It sounds like baby limpkins are in the jungle behind us—which is so dense we wondered how early pioneers made a way through it.

May 26, 1987—

I've been singing a hymn all day that the Lord sent early this morning: "I've Found a Friend, O, Such a Friend" – "he loved me ere I knew him; he drew me with the cords of love, and thus he bound me to him; and round my heart still closely twine those ties which naught can sever, for I am his and he is mine, forever and forever." The third verse adds, "*The eternal glories gleam afar to nerve my faint endeavor,* so now to watch, to work, to war, and then to rest forever."

May 27, 1987—

Last night we stayed at Smokemont Campground in Smoky Mountain National Park. It was very dark, so even after my eyes became adjusted to the dark, it was *still dark.* But the Lord sent visions anyway. One was of intricately patterned pillars to a building. Then I saw a woven cloth that appeared to be fine linen, rather off-white toward the gold plus many shades of green. Yesterday, during a hike, we saw so many varied shades of green in vegetation, I remembered thinking how beautiful it was. The visions of greens last night reminded me that the Lord is in charge of all that is—including the varieties of green.

Today I was more than two miles from camp headed out further when I heard a rumble. Looking up I saw swirling black clouds so turned back toward camp, walking fast. Even at that, it took 45 minutes. I prayed and sang in the Spirit the whole distance and on the last dozen steps before entering the camper, I felt a few drops of rain. When I was inside, fully protected, the heavens opened and the rain poured. The Lord is guarding us so completely and utterly.

The stream of consciousness thoughts that used to roll through my mind—one after another, usually undisciplined, disjointed, unconnected, some negative, some positive—have become more disciplined and centered on Christ. I sing, pray, recite Psalms, think about the Lord and his goodness, think positive thoughts, pray for people, work on theological problems, rejoice frequently, laugh often, look at the sky and its purity and rejoice even more. Praise God!

This morning, I woke to a bright light behind my eyes and the words from John 1:9-13: *The true light, which enlightens everyone, was coming into the world. He was in the world, and the world came into being through him; yet the world did not know him. He came to what was his own, and his own people did not accept him. But to all who received him, who believed in his name, he gave power to become children of God, who were born, not of blood or of the will of the flesh or of the will of man, but of God.*

In the night, the Lord sent a brief vision of a marble wall with a design on it. I do not yet know what it means.

May 31, 1987—

What beautiful days we have been experiencing in these Smoky Mountains! Every morning I waken to a concert of warbler songs floating in the camper windows. This morning I leaped out of bed, grabbed a bite of breakfast and hurried out the door to the forest trails. The heavy dew of morning reflected light from buttercups and violets, making them appear brighter than usual.

A Blackburnian warbler was singing from the top of a tall spruce. I studied that treetop for many minutes without seeing him, but later in the day the Lord sent one into plain view for us. Blackburnian warblers frequent the same areas of forest as the Canada and black-throated blue warblers, and we saw all of these near the same lofty primitive campground called Balsam

Mountain. It was as though God sent them out in the open over our path so we could see them well. Tiny brown creepers were singing there also, surprisingly like winter wrens—so high-pitched and tinkly.

While walking along a trail, we were showered with the delicate petals of mountain laurel and marveled at the loveliness of blooming trees and shrubs—some of which were far from human eyes, but are a reflection of the fruitfulness of God's creation, symbolizing God's abundant grace.

Last night, the Lord sent another strange vision of precious stones in a pattern—first as lines on a plain surface, then the stones filled in the pattern gradually. The whole process took possibly 15 seconds, then disappeared.

Tonight, however, I have discovered the meaning of all these visions. The Bible study lesson I am working on is a detailed description of Solomon's life and the temple he built—its columns, walls and implements. Through these visions of the last few days, God is showing me some of *the glory of Solomon at his greatest time.*

The Lord has started calling me "my daughter" instead of "child".

June 4, 1987–

This morning I awakened to a vision of a crown of gold, followed by bright stars, then symbolic stars sketched in a golden strip. Was this more about Solomon?

June 11, 1987–

Arriving home again, I called Sandra Miller but she was unresponsive because she was angry about my letter. She did not accept any premise of it, so the Lord said to write an addendum to the earlier letter, explaining some things in greater detail.

Dear Sandra,

I still love you and pray for you daily.

The Lord told me to write you again and tell you that he loves you very much – more than you can possibly understand – and promises to lead and guide you to himself. He is and will continue to help you but you are to commit your life to him alone because your own efforts avail nothing.

God says he gave his prophecy of the coming Messiah in many places in Scripture, but the most explicit is in Isaiah: *But he was wounded for our transgressions, crushed for our iniquities; upon him was the punishment that made us whole, and by his bruises we are healed. All we like sheep have gone astray; we have all turned to our own way, and the Lord has laid on him the iniquity of us all* (53:5-6).

He says you are right that the Kingdom of God comes with the Messiah. *It has come in the hearts* of those who accept the Messiah. I am happier than I have ever been in my life. The Lord visits me frequently at night when it is dark. He comes in as a cloud, a sort of fog, lighting up the whole bedroom with the glorious light of his presence. I do not see a person, but one night after I had worked for him all day, the Lord woke me at three by pouring a heavy fog or smoke in the bedroom window filling the whole room as a pink glow permeated the fog bank.

I was so awestruck I shook. The Lord of all that is came to me in the fire and cloud of Moses to confirm my Christian faith. Can't you see that the two faiths are the same?! Christianity is the culmination of the faith of Abraham, Jacob, Moses and Elijah. We are sisters in the same faith! The God of all the universe is your God and mine! He is the one who speaks to me, comforting me in my affliction, raising me up by giving me the gifts of love, peace and joy in response to faith and trust in him.

May this Lord bless you and keep you. May his face shine upon you and give you peace. If you are feeling the touch of God as the result of my prayers, we are in touch with the same God. I still love you.

D.G.

The Lord said, "Haste," so I sent the letter to Sandra. I am praying she will receive it in the spirit of love.

June 14, 1987—

Today at church I began to see a return of the pink glow around the chancel. By this the Lord is showing that daily prayers in the chapel are reaping benefits for the church.

We also attended early church by automobile in the big shopping center parking lot. Pastor Charlie, the young associate, said that God cares about the smallest detail of our lives, and at that exact instant I saw a tiny gnat walking across the windshield between my eye and Charlie's face. God must have sent the gnat to illustrate the sermon. Praise him! On opening the Bible to look up the morning scripture, it fell open to the exact page of the reading. Howard saw this also.

June 15, 1987—

What an exciting night! I could not sleep for hours. When I went to the bathroom, there seemed to be a green light on everything. The light had a pattern across it like small waves drawn by a child to resemble water. Later, it grew in intensity so that the whole bedroom was covered with green waves. *"The Crystal Sea"* in Revelation came to mind.

Then I began to make out an oval of light in the west window—a quarter of its width and longer vertically than horizontally. As I watched it, the head of a *cow* appeared, then I saw horns on the cow. That disappeared and the head of a *lion* flashed in the oval, then the face of a *man*, then an *eagle*. I am not absolutely certain in which order these appeared but I knew they represented the four living creatures spoken of in Revelation that were in the midst of the crystal sea.

Above the oval and to the right flashed the image of *a white lamb* with its head turned toward me. I immediately hopped out of bed, fell to my knees and prayed asking forgiveness. The hymn "It is Well With My Soul" came to mind.

I returned to bed and in the picture oval a baby appeared upside down, as though about to be born. At the same time a bright light shined in the lower part of the window. Then the beautiful purple color I have come to know as from God covered the baby and moved down to encircle the bright light. When the color moved away from the baby, the baby disappeared. The message must be that God was in Jesus as a human baby and that he became the light of the world.

Then I saw the purple color concentrate at the top of the window with bright points of light (stars) which began to shake and fall. *And the stars of the sky fell to the earth as the fig tree drops its winter fruit when shaken by a gale* (Rev 6:13).

I thought about Revelation and looked for a scroll and horses but didn't see them. What a fantastic vision! Then I said, "Lord, speak to me!"

He answered, through a silent inner voice, "You are one of the elect!"

June 18, 1987–

Waves of deep purple, reddish-orange and golden white light rolled into the room again last night. The color was so intense it looked like a liquid. When it was at its peak, it seemed to touch me. The whole sequence of colors occurred one after another with one color dominating a few seconds, then receding to be overtaken by the wave of another color. This continued for about ten minutes. Time is hard to gauge.

After it passed, I went to sleep. Then it felt as though someone were shaking me gently. I awakened to find the window covered with a kaleidoscope of brilliant colored lights, constantly in motion. Sometimes the window would be green, sometimes a soft orange-red. The colors appeared pebbly and were overpoweringly intense. Then the light went out and at the upper left corner of the window flashed a very intense white light with tiny rays radiating out of it in a 360° circle. It was brief—less than a second.

I went to church to pray today. As I sat in the chapel looking at the stained glass windows, it occurred to me that artists who first created stained glass windows must have had visions similar to mine. Where, I wonder, would this be recorded?

June 23, 1987—

We had company for a few days and I have been quite tired by nightfall. Nevertheless the last three nights a quiet fog has come into the bedroom. One night I asked for angels and after some ten minutes, the whole room was bathed in a glorious, emerald-green light which touched me. I felt the embrace of the Spirit. Last night I asked for angels at the windows to guard us, and after a bit, both windows showed green light. Amazing!

June 24, 1987—

Last night there was no color at all, but a strange thing happened to the light in the window. As I was praying, the light became fragmented and appeared as though something separated the light into pieces surrounded by dark even scallops. Then a huge wave of something unseen enveloped me and I felt as though I might be drawn outside of myself. I was not frightened and it passed.

June 25, 1987—

On the way home from praying at the church, I passed a man in a motorized wheelchair. The Lord suggested I stop and pray for him. I protested that it is hard to accost a stranger in this manner. The Lord responded that the Cross was hard too. After circling the block three times, I stopped and told the man the Lord had asked me to stop and pray for him. I also told him the Lord had healed a cancer on my head and had placed a cross there as a sign that I am his. I asked him if he prayed, and he said he did. He held out his hands to me and I gave a simple prayer of praise to God and a request for healing. We exchanged names and I went home.

June 26, 1987—

In the night I saw colored patterns in pink, blue and lime-green. These were human-type colors—like dress design fabrics or curtains or aprons—so clear and lovely. My eyes were closed but when I opened them, the whole room turned blue. The light coming in the window was also blue. Looking at the window, I saw *human faces* in a row across the top—as though someone had taken a dark pencil and sketched them across the light. I looked at the other window and they were there also. They were not angels, because when I call for angels, the Lord sends waves of emerald-green light into the room. When my face lights up, the light is always blue. So the faces represented human faces. The Holy Spirit brought to mind the crowds of people praising God in Revelation 5:11. It seems the Lord is playing Revelation right before my eyes at night—unfolding it as it happened to John who wrote it. But the unfolding to me is in pencil sketches, as it were, not living color.

June 29, 1987—

For some reason, I am becoming more sensitive to beauty. Music, beautiful scenes, good food, smiles and touches of friends evoke powerful feelings. When one confines one's

stimulation to goodness and truth and beauty instead of negativity and evil, life takes on an intensity undreamed of. Paul
said in Philippians: *Finally, beloved, whatever is true, whatever
is honorable, whatever is just, whatever is pure, whatever is pleasing, whatever is commendable, if there is any excellence and if
there is anything worthy of praise, think about these things* (4:8).

A message came to both Miriam and me separately during
the night that a planeload of people we know would not return
from a tour to Rome. Some of these people have made themselves my enemies and have also turned away from Miriam. I
asked for confirmation and the Bible opened to Malachi 4:1:
*"See, the day is coming, burning like an oven, when all the arro-
gant and all evildoers will be stubble; the day that comes shall
burn them up," says the Lord of hosts.* Miriam and I are in shock
about it. What should we do? Some of these folks are innocent
of any wrong against us or the Lord. We are praying about it
and asking for guidance.

While Miriam and I were together, we went to the children's ward of the hospital and prayed for three sick and injured children.

Hazel said I should place a prayer cloth under my pillow so
I praised God while holding a small bottle of olive oil, put
some on handkerchiefs and placed them under our pillows. It
then occurred to me that Delilah, the multiple sclerosis victim,
needed this Spirit vessel to keep with her at all times, so tonight Howard and I took it over, prayed with her, and gave it
to her to take on vacation.

July 2, 1987—
Miriam and I are still concerned about the impending doom
to the crew who will travel to Rome. We discussed whether to

warn them, but then the Bible opened by chance to Luke 22:67, the passage where Jesus tells his captors they will not believe who he is even if he tells them. So he is saying they will not believe our warning. We asked the Lord what to do.

I went to the mall, walked and prayed. While there I received three messages about this problem. One was a hymn: "I'm Praying For You"; one was a word from my friend the popcorn man to pray for them; and the last was a direct message for me to pray. So Miriam and I are praying, separately and together, asking the Lord to have mercy on the innocent. We will leave them to God.

What strange and beautiful visions the Lord sent last night after Miriam and I prayed for the safety of those who would make themselves our enemies. First, I learned the Crystal Sea in Revelation 4:6 is clear glass without color. Shortly after retiring, I lay quietly with my eyes open and began to see the room fill with a band of clear glass, stationary scallops. It looked like the most beautiful cut glass I have ever seen. In wonderment I watched as the facets shone in amazing clarity and brilliance. What a God! I used to speculate about John's Crystal Sea in Revelation. I thought it meant the water was crystal clear. But no, the Crystal Sea in heaven around the throne of God is *magnificent cut glass!*

That wasn't all. Red flames of the Holy Spirit again filled my window, changing to deep purple, green, blue, cream, gold, ruby-red and burnt-orange. At one time the colors gathered themselves into a *straight-line* rainbow across the window. For some reason every time the Lord sends a vision of a rainbow, it is in a straight line. After the rainbow faded, I saw a *whirling wheel* which extended from one side of the window to the other—about 30 inches in diameter. It had an axle and spokes but no rim and it whirled around, sometimes clockwise and sometimes counter-clockwise.

This phenomenon is reported in both Ezekiel and Daniel and is made manifest when the *Lord God of the universe is present!* While this was happening, I felt the embrace of the Holy Spirit giving me a warm, tingly feeling from head to toe. Out of the corner of my eye, *I saw a sparkling spirit beside my bed.* It was a cloud with brilliant sequins on it in the shape of a person. At that time I felt myself start to be drawn out of my body and wondered where I would go, but the feeling passed. Again I was not afraid.

These visions happened between ten and one last night and I saw them with my eyes open. After this the fog of the Lord entered the room, filling it so that when I thrust my hand out, it disappeared in the fog. My body became warm all over, including my head which generally does not receive the heat of the Holy Spirit. In the midst of the fog, I said, "Jesus, come and live with me," and felt another warm surge. Sleep came only when I was too exhausted to stay awake.

July 3, 1987 –

I saw the face of Jesus last night. It started with flames and other colored light coming in the window. Being very tired, I said, "Lord, I am going to sleep a while. Wake me if something is going on I need to see."

He said, "No, wait," so I lay and watched the colors change, the occasional flashes of light in the room and the ever-present fog or cloud of the Lord form as a haze in the entire room with thicker clumps in places. I started drifting to sleep but something shook me awake. The west window began getting lighter and foggier. I looked at the curtain and all at once the image of a figure in a robe appeared. I could see the way the robe was wrapped around the figure and could make out folds in the cloth. The place where the face would be was quite light, but no face was visible.

I prayed and praised God and as though in response, a great wave of fog came in the window. This was lighted with an amber glow and came toward me, then disappeared. Other waves came, each one more intense than the last. Again at one point I felt as though I would be pulled out of my body, but the sensation passed. Just in case, I hopped out of bed, knelt and asked forgiveness for my sins.

Back in bed, I saw that the picture of the robed figure on the curtain was gone. I looked at the other window. In the upper right-hand corner patches of light—yellow started concentrating, then a clear emerald green, then shades of purple that became more intense until there was an indescribably intense, clear-violet light of exquisite beauty. In the middle of it, *I saw the face of Jesus.* It was like a charcoal sketch within the purple. His eyes were closed and the sketch looked like the shroud of Turin painting of Christ by Curtis Hooper. The nose was long, eyes deep-set. It was gone in an instant and all light and color faded. "Whew!" I said, "My Lord and my God!"

July 14, 1987 –

What astonishing visions I had last night at my sister's house. The Lord keeps sending lessons to me by night visions.

Betty and I have always been able to talk about anything and recently I have been telling her a few of the visions the Lord has sent. During the evening, I read to her from Kenneth Hagin's book, *The Anointing.* He related that the Lord allowed him to descend to hell in spirit during his illness before he was healed by the Lord and became a minister. His description of hell was terrifying and Betty and I discussed it at length.

My head had barely touched the pillow when I saw lights and colors swirling about the room. On the ceiling, I began to see a radiance circulating around a central spot. The ceiling disappeared from that site and I could see a great distance into space with a powerful, bright beam at the end. Rays of light shot out of that space and circled my hands. I looked at them and they were flashing with light rays and flames. I briefly put my hands on my tired hurting eyes to ease them. When I next looked at the ceiling, the whirlwind of light was gone but not the visions. I saw a horizontal fence separating what was above from the dark beneath, and faces in agony were passing from above to below the fence. They looked like white masks with mouths open in a scream. A written message appeared at fence level, but alas I could not make out a single word.

Later in the night, I awakened and went to the bathroom. Passing the mirror, I looked in and saw my face radiate with the blue light that I am becoming accustomed to seeing. But something was different. *Small blue bubbles* were floating at random around the room. Someone told me to stay at the mirror. As I watched, still in the dark, I saw my face change to *a youthful face!* I kept thinking Jesus might appear in the mirror and I did see a face behind me in the background briefly, but was told in my inner being that it was Amersa, my angel protector. It's hard to describe the awe I felt. I had to hold onto the lavatory to steady my knees that were about to give way. I went back to bed but it was hours later when sleep came. [The "youthful face" phenomenon is described in Job 33:23-28, when God sends a ransom to restore to man righteousness and youthful vigor.]

July 17, 1987—

Again last night I saw the throne of God. At the top of the window, beautiful jewels played across the scene. Every color of the rainbow in sparkling stones made patterns across the top of the window. Beneath them sat the throne which looked like an ordinary chair with a tall back and high armrests. From the seat flowed brilliant colored lights, culminating in the bright purple I have come to know as God's color. As the color clarified, I saw a scroll in the seat and to the right of the scroll, a white lamb.

These visions were brief—only until I could recognize what they were. Then I saw a galloping horse. [In the June 15 entry I wondered where the scroll and horses of Revelation were so the Lord accommodated and sent one of each.] At one time I felt the embrace of the Spirit over my total being and knew something marvelous was happening and that one day relating these visions would strengthen the faith of others and possibly bring some to a first encounter with Christ.

July 18, 1987—

I am in Oklahoma City attending a mission study. Today I spoke up for the Lord in the seminar on the book of Acts. The teacher, Dr. Robert Lester, offered some farfetched explanations for Pentecost, denying the Word.

I challenged him, citing my friend Jenny's experience of speaking tongues in Spanish to a Mexican in Disney World. The man had asked for directions, and Jenny did not know enough Spanish to answer him but wanted to help. So she began to pray in the Spirit, and *in the Spirit, she gave him instructions he needed in his own language.*

She confirmed this later when she and her family saw the

same man with a friend who knew English and he told the story back to them from the viewpoint of the Mexican. Praise God. But Dr. Lester said he didn't believe it.

July 19, 1987–

I heard today at this seminar of the Russian celebration of the 1,000th year of Christianity and their claim that the color red stands for God, while blue stands for humans. It is logical that the purple light I have seen indicates the spiritual presence of Jesus—a combination of red and blue for divine and human.

Someone said the first hour of a Russian Orthodox service causes the feet to hurt, the second hour brings on a headache, but the third hour lifts the spirit to a heavenly realm of joy and peace. The incense, music, prayers and chanting—and all the people raising their voices in praise—bring to earth a fragment of the kingdom of heaven that worshipers are able to feel.

July 20, 1987–

The Lord has sent many comforting messages today as we traveled across Kansas showing us in several ways that he is with us. He arranged for us to meet, pray with and comfort a woman and child in a restaurant in a small Colorado town.

Many times a day the Lord sends trembling lips indicating I am to pray in the Spirit and I do—sometimes silently and with my mouth closed. This is not always easy, but if the Lord sends it when I am in a conversation, the Spirit prayer has to be silent and take place in another part of the consciousness.

July 21, 1987–

I must write Dr. Lester and be kind, but tell him some things he doesn't know.

Dear Dr. Lester,

I am the one who contended with you concerning Pentecost at the Women's Mission Study last weekend. I am writing at the request of the Lord, who said to my spirit that I should tell you in loving kindness some of the things he has caused to happen to me. It is also to his credit, not mine, that I returned to your class on Saturday and again on Sunday.

My closeness with the Lord started five years ago when my best friend died. The Lord knew my grief so he sent to my ear the wonderful sound of bells ringing and told me that my friend was in heaven ringing the joy bells. The Lord has been close to me since then and has healed me from cancer, kidney failure, appendicitis, pneumonia and numerous smaller problems. He has responded favorably to my prayers for healing of others – though not all. My faith still has a long way to go.

Two years ago the Lord sent me the gift of tongues. This came as I knelt alone to say my prayers at my own bedside and in the manner I described in the Pentecost paper. My lips trembled, my tongue felt thick, my flesh felt electrified and my mouth started whispering strange sounds that I cannot interpret. The language continued while I was on my knees for a while; then I went in another room, where it continued for about an hour.

The phenomenon did not recur for several weeks – and then only in partial strength. But it is still sent by the Lord from time to time. My lips start twitching in a characteristic manner to initiate every episode. This happened Friday in your class when you presented some alternative suggestions to explain Pentecost. The Spirit could not stand those apostasies. I do not remember what I said, but that message was from the Lord, as is this one.

I always read 1 Corinthians 13 to exercise gifts of the Spirit in love before reading the next chapter about the practical applications. Paul says in 14:28: *let them ... speak to themselves and to God* if there is no interpretation. In verse 33 he explains: *for God is a God not of disorder but of peace.* Whatever the language is, it speaks to the Spirit under the stimulus of the Spirit. When there is a motive of love and caring for others, a "tongue" can appear as a distinct language as happened at Pentecost where strangers from many countries heard Christ preached in their own languages. This happened to my friend Jenny when she asked God to help her give assistance to the Mexican in Florida. Jenny is a dedicated, committed Christian who lives her whole life in devotion to God. She does not lie and her husband and children were witnesses to the episode.

I used to be a chemist and because of that training believed that everything that happened was scientifically provable or would be when people learned all of the natural laws. If something was not logical, it didn't happen. Not until I was beyond 55 years of age did I learn that spiritual laws supersede physical laws. When spiritual laws are more true than the physical ones, the spiritual event occurs. This happened often in "the Word" and can and does happen today. Many times, however, it is not spoken of except by the bravest because the enlightener is often ridiculed.

When there is a powerful service of worship, I sometimes see flickering tongues of flames of the Holy Spirit in the place of praise. That occurred in the chapel during the opening session when the congregation rose in a powerful hymn of praise.

The Lord is still with us and is still accessible to help the ones who faithfully call on his name, trust him, love him and obey him. He loves you and calls you to preach his Word to a lost people.

Yours in Christ,
D.G.

July 23, 1987—

The Lord confirmed his instructions for me to write the above letter by opening the Bible to 2 Timothy: *Do not be ashamed, then, of the testimony about our Lord ...* (1:8). Also, the hymn, "O Zion, Haste," came, indicating I should copy the letter and mail it. So I did. [There was no answer.]

July 25, 1987—

After reading Kenneth Hagin's book on faith, I decided to take Jesus at his Word that we are healed by his stripes (1 Pet

2:24), so I stopped taking the blood pressure medicine. Late that night I wakened with pulse racing and head pounding. I got up and took the medicine, apologizing to the Lord for my weak faith. This morning I was surprised to see a vision of a black and white checkered "winner" flag. Later the Lord sent the hymn, "We Shall Overcome Someday." [I now see that we should *not* avoid doctors or stop taking medicine until the Lord or the doctors tell us to. Unless the manifestation of healing is complete, we should not give up on our medicine.]

July 27, 1987–

I hiked this morning in the beautiful spruce and mixed deciduous forest of Wolf Creek camping area in Colorado. The wild flowers were lovely, especially as seen through a four-power portrait lens. Blue flax buttered the meadow next to the campground; wild roses sprang up near damp ditches; and monkshoods were mixed with chiming bells in a high marsh. Many young birds were cheeping—evening grosbeaks, golden-crowned kinglets, chipping sparrows and gray-headed juncos. I could hear the beautiful cascading trill of the canyon wren on the red cliffs beside the stream.

After hiking about a mile upstream I sat on a rock, prayed and sang to the Lord. A goshawk and a sharp-shinned hawk flew over my head sometime during the morning. I felt secure and comforted with the hymn "I Know That My Redeemer Liveth" running through my head. The sky was a pure cerulean blue and the clear mountain runoff stream made melody over the rocks. Howard was downstream watching an American dipper and we both found spotted sandpipers along this stream many miles from any sandy beach.

At one point I asked the Lord to make the future easy, then

as I watched, a quaking aspen nearby shook its leaves in the flickering I am accustomed to seeing when the Holy Spirit is present. The quaking stopped as soon as I had acknowledged it. The Lord is so good.

A picket fence is appearing many times in visions. Last night it was absolutely dark in the camper. I closed my eyes and soon came the swelling lights of the Spirit world beyond the pale (death). The pale is the fence I have been seeing by the side of every vision. When I opened my eyes, the vision was still there. To the side of the picket fence, I saw rays of light flash out of the center of the color mass, a ball, and hit my face. I feel as though I were living in the kingdom of heaven right now.

July 29, 1987–

We are camped in the lovely little valley of Ouray, Colorado. It has been a splendid trip so far. Everything has progressed very well; we know the Lord is with us. I have seen Howard smiling and so happy on this trip. He has a beautiful smile.

Last night we prayed for the campground host whose hearing is failing. He visited us in our camper and we laid hands on him and prayed. I don't know if he has faith in the prayer or not, but I will continue to pray for him.

Today the Lord sent the hymn "Savior, More Than Life to Me" all day. "I am clinging close to thee; let thy precious blood applied, keep me ever near thy side. Let me love thee more and more, till this fleeting life is o'er; till my soul is lost in love, in a brighter world above. Every day, every hour, Let me feel Thy cleansing power; may Thy tender love to me bind me closer, Lord, to thee."

July 30, 1987–

This morning we spoke to a neighbor in the trailer park but

he only looked at us and did not speak. For some reason I thought he might have emphysema. Tonight the Lord said to go visit him. I knocked and when he opened the door, I spoke to him but he couldn't understand what I said. He was deaf and handed me a paper and pen so I wrote, asking if I might pray for his hearing. He smiled and agreed. I went in, put my hands on his ears and prayed that God would restore his hearing. I wrote him a note asking if he believed in Jesus, and he said he did. Since then, I have prayed for his hearing again and again.

August 2, 1987—

We rented a jeep for two days and explored the high mountains by way of old mining and timber roads. One jeep trail we explored was so scary I rode white-knuckled the whole way. Stretches of trail were narrow, steep and slippery; and at these times the Lord sent trembling lips to indicate I should pray, so I did, both in English and in the Spirit tongue. I'm sure angels helped us to make it. When we had returned in safety, I resolved never to ride on those trails again.

August 4, 1987—

I am learning splendid truths from Kenneth Hagin's book, *The Name of Jesus.* He says and proves by Scripture that we are Christ's body on earth—almost legalistically so—and we are to repeat what he did using his name, and it shall be done for us. We have Jesus' "power of attorney." Fantastic! All we have to do is acquire the mind of Christ, plus his compassion and love; forgive our enemies, commit ourselves to studying and digesting the word, give up fear, be bold to speak for Christ in every situation; then God will do miracles for our asking. We are to intercede for others (including our president and our country) and order Satan out of their lives and claim them for Christ.

August 7, 1987—

Today at the altitude of the Cloudcroft, New Mexico campground, about 9,000 feet, I hiked a couple miles in the morning and another three this afternoon. Approaching the ski trail from the backside of the mountain, I walked a long ways in a high meadow with no sign of the morning trail. As I started i[the side of the mountain I asked, "Lord, is this the right way back?" He said, "Yes."

I then asked, "Send a hymn," and immediately, he sent "He Leadeth Me." Soon he said to turn around. I did and saw a familiar view from this morning, so the two trails connected and I was safely climbing the mountain on a now obvious trail. When near the safety of camp, I sat on a log and prayed for a long time, feeling so close to the Lord. He had walked with me along that trail, encouraging me at every juncture.

Yesterday morning I was at a K.O.A. Laundromat when a woman entered complaining of mosquito bites on her ankle. I suggested we pray for the insect-bitten flesh to stop itching and heal. She agreed and I stooped, touched her ankles and prayed aloud. Though we were both in that place another half-hour, she never complained again.

August 9, 1987—

The Lord is sending visions of the next day's events. Two nights ago the vision consisted of evergreen trees against the sky. The next day on a hike, I saw that scene when I looked up. Last night the vision showed rain. Sure enough, rains came in the night to cool the desert that we were to pass through.

August 10, 1987—

Again last night the Lord sent swelling colors to my window. In the midst of this program, I saw three bright pinpoints of light move together to make one ball of light. It was coming from the middle of a sheet of rich violet light. I accepted the meaning to be the three-in-one of the Trinity of God. Also the cloud of the Lord came in the window and hovered over the bed. What fantastic visions the Lord is granting me! When the cloud faded, I looked at the ceiling and called the name "Jesus." Immediately the form of a person in a white robe appeared above me in the air! It was extremely brief, then the cloud of the Lord closed in again.

August 15, 1987–

Praise the Lord! Marie, the little lady my sister and I prayed for, went to the doctor, and *he couldn't find any trace of cancer in her lungs.* She was ecstatic when she called my sister. We also are overjoyed. God is so good!

August 16, 1987–

Last night, the Lord was powerfully present in this room, sending a vision of translucent colored stones, jewels and then a platform with three steps going up to a throne. Only light was on the throne—a blinding light.

August 19, 1987–

We are at Cape Hatteras, North Carolina, after flying to Norfolk, Virginia, renting a car and driving south. I'm convinced the pattern of events today followed the Lord's plan. Last night the Lord sent a vision of a crater, like the backside of the moon. On the plane today I was looking through *The Atlantic* magazine and discovered an article on the volcanic crater in northern Arizona. The picture shown in the magazine was a replica of my vision. What an amazing visitation!

A charming little ten-year old girl, Rebecca, sat beside us on the plane. We talked and said a blessing together over lunch.

August 22, 1987 –

We have ridden in a 50-foot diesel engine powerboat on the Atlantic Ocean for two days. This was why we came here—to spot ocean birds we had never seen before. The first day was so rough, I thought about not going today, but changed my mind and it turned out to be a splendid day. We found our sea legs and identified several new species for our life list. We watched pilot whales and bottle-nosed porpoises in pods—diving, jumping and playing around the boat. We even glimpsed a giant sunfish, over six feet long and thin as your hand.

Yesterday one man got seasick. He looked so white and ill as he lay on a bench in the cabin, I asked if I might pray for him. He said it couldn't hurt so I laid a hand on his clammy forehead and prayed. He kept getting better as the day progressed and was all right by the time we started back to land.

I spent two hours sitting in the stern of the boat praying as we cruised to the gulf stream. Part of the prayer was asking the Lord to post angels around the boat to keep us safe. Soon he sent a hymn with angels mentioned in it to assure us he had heard the prayer, and it was accomplished.

How can one adequately describe the beauty of peacefully cruising over deep water in the early morning, watching the sky change to reds and pinks and yellows as the sun rises, seeing gulls and terns overhead—soaring and plunging over the clear water. The color of the ocean changes to a deep aquamarine in the 100-fathom-plus depth of the Gulf Stream. Continental shelf water is a slightly different shade, though it appears as clear as the Gulf Stream—which is 80° F—as is the air temperature. I had a longing to jump out of the boat and swim, but sharks were around so we weren't allowed out of the boat.

I overheard the leaders discussing the trip and they said they hoped the bird-watchers appreciated the fair weather, the soft waves and the abundance of birds we saw on the trip. They commented it was an unusual trip to have so many factors perfect. I laughed to myself and praised the Lord. One woman asked if I had prayed for the birds to appear. I said I had prayed but was leaving the details to God. I pursued the subject of the Lord, but she walked away and avoided me after that.

August 26, 1987—

Two days ago in Manteo, North Carolina, I awakened thinking the Lord said "living table." I thought this meant the church we were going to attend would be having Communion, but not so. In the afternoon, we visited the local aquarium with its living fish, sharks and shellfish in tanks. Perhaps the message meant we would see edible fishes alive. Also, not so. Two days later Bob Deerfield told the story of the exhausted migrant song birds that land on the dry Tortugas, west of Key West, which are so sluggish from fatigue that predator hawks circle by the hundreds to catch their prey without effort—like *a living table.*

August 27, 1987—

After praying intently in the early evening, I turned out the light and went to bed. A cloud entered the room, covering my hands so I couldn't see them. Lights and pink flickering flames radiated from the cloud around my hands. They began to burn with the fire of the Holy Spirit. I praised God. It seems incredible that *the creator of the universe* is coming to visit a mortal with feet of clay, showing me some of the glories of heaven!

When the cloud lifted, tiny bubbles of rainbow colors covered everything in the room. Later I saw a vision of the head of a dragon—a blood-red head—in the attitude of anger with flared nostrils and gleaming eyes. That was only a very brief moment.

Another time that night I saw a man's face. The Lord said it was my angel, Amersa. There were light flashes, movement, bright pinpoints of light—once in the form of a cross. What awesome sights the Lord is allowing me! Praise him!

As the Psalmist says, *If you try my heart, if you visit me by night, if you test me, you will find no wickedness in me; my mouth does not transgress. ... As for me, I shall behold your face in righteousness; when I awake I shall be satisfied, beholding your likeness* (17:3, 15).

August 28, 1987—

The Lord is now supplying protection for us that I can see. One night I saw a white vapor or spirit with no particular form outside the window. Immediately the window took on bars and crosspieces to indicate the bedroom was barred against evil spirits so I knew that we were being protected. Then the whole window from top to bottom flashed with a sheet of red flames of the Holy Spirit. O, Father, thank you for your presence.

August 30, 1987—

The visions from the Lord took a different turn last night. As I looked at the window, one pane became a sort of television screen first with waves and light flickers on the screen and then a clear picture of people fleeing from something. I thought about Revelation and determined to read it again. Several spirits seemed to be present. I asked if Amersa were here and received a spiritual hug. Later in a corner of the window appeared a small moving figure with wings. Could it be a cherub?

August 31, 1987–

Today the Lord saved me from an automobile accident. I changed lanes and nearly ran over a car that had approached fast from my blind spot. Miraculously, *our cars did not even touch!* Angels held them apart. Praise God! He told me yesterday that he protects us not only from diseases and natural tragedies, but also from accidents.

September 4, 1987–

What an awesome vision of the wheels of Ezekiel was visited upon me last night! This time they were four-sided, each side a whirling wheel with spokes but no rim. Inside the four wheels shone *light* and *fire.* I must review the scriptural wheels and see what they symbolize.

The Lord revealed to me that Miriam's intercession with him saved the tour group traveling to Rome last month. She had pleaded with him for mercy and he gave them a reprieve. I had prayed also, and they did come home safely.

I told the Lord I would like to hear a song or voice from heaven, so in the middle of the night I heard a human tenor voice sing one note—only one. It lasted possibly five seconds.

September 5, 1987–

I visited Rose tonight. She is gaining in faith every day, though her body is failing. I prayed with her, and she didn't want to release my hand.

Last night the Lord awakened me with the hymn "Rescue the Perishing, Pray For the Dying." Immediately I offered up a prayer for people that were dying and interceded, asking God's forgiveness for them. Today he sent the hymn "Christ Arose" to confirm my prayer.

September 11, 1987 –

Today the message came that a dear old friend died. I had visited Joseph within the last two weeks, but had been forbidden to pray aloud for him. I did hug him and in the course of the conversation mentioned the Lord and told about Marie's healing from lung cancer.

I hope someone else watered the seeds I planted. At least when I prayed for him, my hands became very hot. This friend must have been the one the Lord had in mind when he asked me last week to pray for the dying. The later message that Christ arose was to say that Joseph was forgiven and would rise from the grave and live in heaven.

During the past week I have been receiving visions of horizontal lines and wondered if it were a ladder into heaven. Today the meaning came clear. I wakened with both Joseph and Rose on my mind and the message, "first balcony." After thinking about it, I decided it meant both Joseph and Rose are or will be in the first balcony of heaven. Thank you, Father.

Yesterday I had the unique experience of holding a chickadee in my hand while it picked a seed out of my palm. What a thrilling experience!

I am beginning to understand the way the world operates. I really believe all evil—including earthquakes, tidal waves, wild fires, severe weather, droughts, epidemics, birth defects, out-of-control populations, starvation, ravaged eco-systems and everything not perfect—is of Satan and caused by evil spirits loosed somehow by sin and evil in the heart of people.

When I am out in the world, God sends trembling lips most of the time to indicate I should pray, because unprotected by the Holy Spirit and angels, anything can happen and frequently does.

October 3, 1987—

In the night, I heard men's voices. I did not hear English or any identifiable language, just a low murmur of deep, male voices in conversation. In the background was a din of sound— like a large crowd of people talking. I sat up in bed to see if it might be coming from a radio left on next door. But *nothing was coming from outside!* The Lord was allowing me *to hear through a crack in heaven!* This type of occurrence is reported in Ezekiel 1:24, *When they moved, I heard the sound of their wings like the sound of mighty waters, like the thunder of the Almighty, a sound of tumult like the sound of an army.*

October 27, 1987—

We drove the camper to Rock Creek State Park today. It is cool and quiet here so we sat in the dark this evening listening to Pavarotti tapes. The window was open and from outside drifted in the odor of ancient rocks and darkness. After going to bed, I heard the flutter of cherub wings in my ear.

Though the wood thrushes and ovenbirds have departed, their summer singing left an aura of joy through these wooded hills. I have felt jubilant as I walked the trails and photographed the closing of the season. Come November the color in the autumn leaves will be gone and so will the visitors. Left to guard this beautiful little valley will be crows and blue jays, bobcats and coyotes and squirrels. And the Lord.

While resting from hikes, I read Ezekiel in the Good News Bible. I grasp eagerly at the verses containing his visions of living creatures and wheels because I have seen the faces of the four living creatures and the whirling wheels. This phenomenon goes with the glory of God. Ezekiel also speaks of flames and clouds and Shekinah glory, the light of the glory of God.

During a nap I experienced a wild dream. First I saw the flickering of the Holy Spirit in a strip of water taken out of the ocean. It was as if a narrow ribbon of water had jumped out of the ocean and was dancing in time with the flickering of the Spirit. Beneath lay the entire ocean where I floated on my back. It was so comfortable and I felt safe, cradled, so to speak, by the Holy Spirit. I started swimming an easy backstroke, then all at once felt myself being pulled upward, drawn high up very swiftly.

I thought, Oh, I'm going to see the Lord. By then the earth was only a tiny ball beneath me. Immediately I stopped going up and started falling down just as quickly. I looked down and saw the ocean far below and wondered mildly if I would hit very hard—but I was not afraid. When I approached the surface of the water, something slowed the descent and set me gently into the sea again. Just then I wakened.

One night I woke up screaming. Howard turned on the light and the only thing I remember seeing then was a ball of green fog like the color of angel wings. Do you suppose an angel of the Lord came to see me and I was too frightened to converse with him?

October 30, 1987–

This morning I asked the Lord, "Why don't you send an angel in the daytime when I am not so frightened?"

He answered, "I do send them but you can't see them in the day, but they protect you from tragedy and guide you on your way." *If you remove the yoke from among you, the pointing of the finger, the speaking of evil, if you offer your food to the hungry and satisfy the needs of the afflicted, then your light shall rise in the darkness and your gloom be like the noonday. The Lord will guide you continually, and satisfy your needs in parched places, and make your bones strong; and you shall be like a watered garden, like a spring of water, whose waters never fail* (Isa 58:9-11).

Rose died last week. I know she must be in heaven because of what the Lord said about Joseph and Rose being in the first balcony of heaven when he was preparing me for Joseph's death. God is merciful.

November 1, 1987—

Earlier this fall I was driving across the state alone one Sunday. Just before eleven the Lord said to stop and attend church. He said, "Now," so I pulled into a church parking lot right off the highway. The church was a denomination I had not attended before. I asked at the door if I might worship with them since I was in slacks and didn't know their regulations. They welcomed me and soon I was in the middle of an Assembly of God worship service. It was simple, moving and Spirit-filled. Prayers in tongues were not loud and clashing, but a low, tuneful murmur. While praying I felt a deep warmth enter my chest. Words that came from my tongue were different than the usual ones the Spirit sends.

The message of the morning was from Jeremiah 1:7-8: *But the Lord said to me, "Do not say, 'I am only a boy'; for you shall go to all to whom I send you, and you shall speak whatever I command you. Do not be afraid of them, for I am with you to deliver you," says the Lord.* I felt that the minister was speaking directly to me for the Lord has many plans for my witness.

We live close to the railroad tracks and whenever a train goes by, the neighborhood dogs cry out and howl to relieve the pain in their ears from the high squeal of wheels against tracks. Lately when I hear a train coming and the dogs howling, I start to pray that God relieve their pain by closing their ears, however he wishes to do it. The howling stops abruptly.

November 5, 1987—

Last night the Spirit did not seem near at first. I asked to see or hear a piece of heaven before I slept. Late in the night I woke and the Lord sent to my closed eyes a vision—intricately cut glass in a pattern around a circle. Then a green color started filling in. I was seeing a shield or ceiling with very beautiful emeralds that glistened in the reflection of God's light. Gazing into the spiritual realm is one of God's special gifts. I do not have words to express the wonder I feel with this gift.

November 12, 1987—

I needed a day out on the prairie. The private ranch I have permission to explore is virgin tall-grass prairie. Bluestems, Indian grass and switch-grass carpet these rolling hills for miles. The view from the top of a hill is almost as soothing to the spirit as repeating the 23rd Psalm.

I saw both Smith's and Lapland longspurs and two Sprague's pipits. The pipits were easily kicked up as I walked along the ridge. I knew they were Sprague's pipits when they flew quite high for a little while, then dropped like a rock to just above the ground before putting out their wings to break the fall. They reminded me of the dream I had of rising to a great height and falling very fast at first, then slowing to drop softly into the ocean. The prairie wind that blows constantly down these slopes felt like the cool breath of God himself.

A tiny LeConte's sparrow, not much bigger than a thumb, squeaked as it darted up out of tall grass, flew in a zigzag pattern for a few feet, then landed and was not seen again. If I were to run to the place it disappeared, it would no longer be there, having walked 20 or 30 or 50 feet on the ground through the thick grasses.

This time of year hawks begin to drift back to the southern prairie for winter feeding after spending the summer months much farther north. I was lucky to see a rough-legged hawk with wide wings and a dark tail-band, circling at mid-day. I walked through tall grasses down a hill to look for short-eared owls. None appeared, but where a few post oaks and blackjacks congregated, I heard the sweet "cheery, cheery" of bluebirds. Anyplace you hear bluebirds is a good place to be. I would not like to see the world destroyed. One day my friend Doris and I decided we really did love the world the way God made it. I can scarcely imagine anything more beautiful than this world.

November 18, 1987—

I have been praying often and tearfully for Gary who is now in a nearby hospital. With the Lord's encouragement I finally went to see him. He was home from the hospital, but it was a 50-mile drive to Tulsa. He was depressed and very ill from multiple sclerosis—paralyzed, non-speaking. He refused to let me pray for him but he did let me read poetry, which brought a smile to his face.

The Lord has spent the last few days right with me, encouraging me in every way to visit Gary, but also he has just been here. He has sent trembling lips many times. I have not known why I was to pray or for whom, but I did pray.

November 21, 1987—

"O rest in the Lord, wait patiently on him and he will give you your heart's desire" is the line of a song the Lord sent this morning. All through the night, every time I was even semi-aware, I either saw the flickering of the Holy Spirit or felt it.

Once I wondered if we were having an earthquake when I felt the whole bed quivering to the rhythm of the flickering flames of the Holy Spirit.

December 14, 1987–

We are in Baton Rouge, Louisiana, after a short trip to northern Florida where we visited Howard's cousin. Late this afternoon in the campground I was sitting in a swing next to the swimming pool. I prayed for a while, then asked the Lord to send an angel to talk to me. After a few minutes a lovely young blond girl, about 17, came out of the campground office and walked my way. I spoke and she stopped. We had hardly begun a conversation when she was called to the telephone at the office.

After she left, I asked the Lord if she were an angel. He said, "Almost." She came again, stopped, and we talked at length. She is a senior in high school, a valedictorian and is taking classes in physics, Spanish, English, higher math, world history and band! What a schedule! She is applying to several colleges but expects to attend L.S.U. which is nearby. She smiled often, said, "Yes, ma'am," and said she was a Baptist. I was taken with her demeanor, her intelligence and her beauty.

Someone called her from their trailer and I walked part way back with her telling her of my asking the Lord to send an angel. Then I asked her name. She said, *"Angela!"*

December 15, 1987–

Today as we were driving across the country, I found myself rattling off praises to the Lord without thinking very much about it. Shortly the Lord sent a vision of a windmill flapping in the breeze without being connected to anything. I laughed and acknowledged my empty-headedness.

Tonight I have had such a joyful feeling without any particular reason to be joyful, except the certainty that the Lord is very close all the time.

I hand-washed a blouse and hung it on the clothesline outside. Wind blew the hanger against a honeysuckle bush where the sleeves wrapped around limbs. Surely, I thought, it would be ruined. But it was perfectly clean and unmarked! As I walked back to the house, the Lord sent a hymn, "Angels From the Realms of Glory," to tell me an angel had kept the blouse from being damaged. God is the Lord of the smallest detail. Bless him!

December 25, 1987—

Today, Christmas, I awakened to flickering red flames next to my pillow. The Lord was sending the Holy Spirit to assure me of his presence, but trembling lips signaling Spirit prayer has not come. Sometime in November, the Lord stopped sending that message. I don't know why.

December 29, 1987—

Last night the Lord sent a vision of fabric designs as he sometimes does to portray human activity. Then came lights and movement in chaotic patterns along with a ferris wheel, or half of one, followed by layers of darkness with human skulls falling. No doubt God was portraying the world under Satan's control which will end with destruction to those who live with worldly values. The message was to continue giving up the evil side of the world and seek the Lord only. God wants us to pursue holiness with all our being.

December 30, 1987—

The Lord sent trembling lips today! Surely the Christmas

season, starting in mid-November, was so stressful I lost my sensitivity and was not able to receive God's instructions.

January 15, 1988 –

We are headed for south Texas for eight weeks. On the trip today I heard a radio minister speak of the necessity of having joy in our hearts in order to realize the power of God. Then the Lord sent the tune "Without a Song." Indeed, life is impossible without a song. Amen and amen.

January 16, 1988 –

This morning the Lord sent the hymn "All Creatures of our God and King" – a song of praise to God for all good things. Actually all good things of the earth *do* praise God as Psalm 103:20-22 says: *Bless the Lord, O you his angels, you mighty ones who do his bidding, obedient to his spoken word. Bless the Lord, all his hosts, his ministers that do his will.* **Bless the Lord, all his works,** *in all places of his dominion. Bless the Lord, O my soul.*

January 22, 1988 –

One night I had a vision of a dome, as seen from underneath, with precious stones around a central point. Sometimes they were one color, sometimes variegated. I have been asking the Lord to place Delilah, my sick friend, here with me in spirit under the dome of the Holy Spirit so she may be healed.

Another night I heard men's voices and a great din in the campground. I looked outside but there was nothing. *It was in my ear only* and coming from heaven or angels. In the midst of all the glory and sounds of heaven, I asked the Lord, "Are you going to give me the gift of prophesy?"

"I already have!" he answered.

February 2, 1988–

The Lord was disappointed in me last night because I failed to witness to Jim Chauser about Jesus. I received another opportunity today. Summoning my courage and asking God's help, I began, telling him that meditation using one's own spiritual energy was a failure because I had tried it for ten years. I told him he needed to pray and meditate to the living God, and Jesus is his name. He said he had not made up his mind about God, then changed the subject.

Jim, a slender young man, about 26, spoke very little, yet when he did, it was "Yes, ma'am," or "No, ma'am." His features were bound in a tight mask that revealed no emotion; we really didn't know what he was thinking. It turned out that he felt comfortable with us and sought us out several times after the first meeting. Later he even told us his dream of traveling to Africa on a shoestring budget to see animals and birds he had never seen before. He gave us his address and I wrote to him from up river at Falcon State Park, Texas.

Dear Jim,

It is raining and very foggy today at Falcon Lake where we are camped in the state park. We have scattered seeds outside near the camper and are seeing pyrrhuloxia, cardinals, green jays, white-crowned sparrows, green-tailed towhees, white-tipped, inca and mourning doves, curve-billed thrashers, cha-chalacas, red-wings, cowbirds, great-tailed grackles, bobwhite and scaled quails. I saw black-throated sparrows yesterday in the thick tangles of brush and cactus. Tomorrow, we are planning to go to Solenino to look for brown jays.

I have thought and thought of a way to suggest to you the meaning and nature of reality as I see it. So here goes. I will tell you what I believe.

The Christian story is awesomely simple. It is the story of God, the creator, who made the world and everything in it and loves it all. God made people giving them intelligence, creativity, ability to develop skills, to love and freedom to choose how they would use these abilities. People chose to use them in the wrong way in that they caused pain and harm to come to other people and creatures, earth and atmosphere, river and ocean. Humans were also disobedient to their creator.

So God sent a special person, a part of his own being, whose name is Jesus, to feed the hungry, heal the sick, comfort the sorrowful, love the unlovely, visit the old and lonely, show people how to live and tell them about God's love for the whole earth.

But the people couldn't stand a perfect person in their midst, so they crucified and killed him. As he was dying, he asked God to forgive them. This forgiveness is still available to all people for all the evil they do, for all time. All you have to do is ask for it.

After three days, Jesus rose from the dead and was seen by over 500 people including his disciples who had fled the cruci- fixion scene in terror. This sight of him alive so convinced them that he was of God, they spent their entire lives telling others about Jesus and his Salvation. They were killed in very horrible ways because of it, but they were no longer afraid.

I myself have not been a committed Christian for very long. God seemed so remote, I didn't see how a man could be God. I tried the yoga meditation (physical and mental yoga) for about ten years. It helped some, but in matters of life and death, it was a failure. One's own spirit, tapped by yoga meditation, is very strong because we have been created in the image of God and naturally have some of God's power and spirit. Under great stress, that human power and spirit folds up and it is necessary to find a power that cannot fail. God's power and spirit through Jesus Christ is failure-proof.

I have used that power, by asking, many times and have received healing for skin-cancer, kidney failure, pneumonia, ap- pendicitis, severe knee injuries, high blood pressure, eye prob- lems and many other lesser problems. The Lord has saved me from automobile accidents, kept fire ants from stinging when I stepped on an ant hill in Florida and had them crawling all over my bare legs. God has healed people I have touched and prayed for. One old lady in Missouri was dying of lung cancer and now, a year later, has no evidence of cancer.

Best of all, I am no longer afraid because I know I am in the protective hands of God who has promised to preserve my soul even when my physical body is dead. I do not think God will ever allow me to be in a position of having to use violence to protect myself because God protects me.

You need that protection, Jim, and that freedom from stress. You have so many plans for seeing and enjoying all of this beautiful world. I'm certain God will go with you and protect you and help you see all of it, but instead of depending on your own programming and good luck, you need to tap in on the creator of all that is. We did not create ourselves or any of the world. It has been intricately and tenderly made. We are loved and cared for by a far greater power than ourselves. You don't have to take my word for it. Just try it. Ask God to help you and ask the Spirit of Jesus Christ to live in you and be with you. Be righteous; love everyone you come in contact with and praise God continually for all your blessings. If any trouble comes toward you, just mention the name of Jesus asking for help and he will send it. When you have hurt anyone, ask forgiveness and your spirit will be restored.

I guarantee it will work. You will feel differently immediately. You will feel great, be rid of all the stress and obsessions and you will love the whole world. I am praying for you. You should feel the results of that.

Your friend,
D.G.

February 13, 1988—

William Barklay has written a two-volume commentary on Revelation, which I have just purchased and read. His historical facts are quite good, but I disagree with his interpretation of the book. He does, however, make one comment that I like very much: When John saw the throne of God, the one seated on the throne was light of the most beautiful colors! Hallelujah! That is what I am seeing in the night—exquisitely beautiful colors of light. How can I doubt the Lord of the universe is with me all the time?

The Lord called my name again last night—an out loud voice that awakened me. No message was delivered, but I felt the peace and assurance of the Holy Spirit.

February 16, 1988 –

The Lord sent a dream of a pet white lamb that kept escaping from the basement where I had it secured for it was trying to come with me. I had too many responsibilities to take it so I locked it in the basement again.

February 20, 1988 –

The Santa Ana National Wildlife Refuge was so pleasant this morning when I took an early walk. Spanish moss hung from many of the live oak trees making a canopy over the trails. An olive or Texas sparrow squeaked from a dense thicket beside the trail with a call closely resembling the sound made by drawing a fingernail across a blackboard. It brought shivers to my body, but I stood still long enough to see it venture out of the brush and scurry across the trail, oblivious of my being there. From a distance a low mournful "Hosea Maria" revealed the presence of white-winged doves, residents of the tropics.

Near the Rio Grande River a kiskadee flycatcher called its name over and over. "Kis-ka-dee," it said, between forays over the river to catch insects. Its colorful red, yellow and black plumage is wild but not gaudy. Only the Master Workman could create such a striking, yet pleasing, contrast. Sections of this riparian refuge are semi-desert with paloverde, cactus and curve-billed thrashers. Hiking through this was comfortable today because it was cool. A light flannel jacket over my shirt was sufficient covering. I took several pictures for a memento and talked to the Lord while stopping to rest.

I began thinking about Eden and the Lord brought to remembrance the time I saw the woods along Sand Creek transformed into a brightly-colored scene that made me gasp because of its beauty.

Then I remembered seeing a double image at other times—as though there were two identical scenes superimposed on one another, one much more brilliantly colored. One must have been physical, the other spiritual. So a "new heaven and a new earth" are the perfect spiritual representations of the physical—that was Eden. The cherubim guard the gates of Eden to keep people from reëntering the spiritual realm, so we glimpse only a fragment of the spiritual realm or Eden where there is a perfection of life without evil of any kind—no violence, no lies, no accidents, no natural catastrophes, no war or hatred, no diseases, and no poverty.

February 21, 1988 –

A strange dream occurred this week. I had thought to ignore it but today I read John and Paula Sanford's *The Elijah Task* and the dream's purpose has been revealed. In the dream I was wielding an ax—actually cutting off a head. It was by instruction. I had to do it—felt no remorse; talked to the person while doing it and did not wake up sorrowful. It was like a play—seeing myself do this thing.

It may be that prophets have at times to wield an ax—perhaps to themselves. The Sanfords say we have to die completely to self to be messengers for God and add that prophets are stripped bare of friends, influence, bodily comforts, pride, popularity and recognition. Prophets frequently fail and fall when beginning, are laughed at, ridiculed, misunderstood and persecuted. They cannot choose to be a prophet but they are chosen by God. Prophets are servants of God. They must do whatever God asks, go wherever he asks, whenever he asks.

February 25, 1988 –

Last evening I attended the Baptist church prayer service in Rio Hondo, Texas where a missionary from Mexico was guest speaker. He is establishing four churches there and asked for volunteers who know Spanish to come and help. The field is open and he spoke so movingly of Christ's love and the need to evangelize Mexico that the entire sanctuary brightened to extremely white light, showing the presence of God. Then fog surrounded his face—the fog of God.

February 29, 1988 –

I was awakened early this morning with the Lord saying to me, "I will show you what is to take place." This message was spoken twice so I would not fail to understand it. Lying quietly with eyes closed, I saw the following scenes. Some were animated, stylized pictures and some like a movie photograph of live action. The scene switched as soon as I understood it.

- A hay mower was cutting wheat in a grain field with blades moving back and forth across each other like an electric hedge clipper.
- Next came a large container–tub or wooden bin–of a grain which looked like corn.
- This was followed by rows of stiff trees or plants shaped like triangles which I perceived were barren.
- A close-up of them showed their fruit to be cockleburs.
- A closer examination highlighted wicked thorns and barbs on these cockleburs.
- The scene faded to darkness, inferring there was no harvest.
- A flashback to the first grain showed a huge white barn with windows.

- Again darkness played across the screen, implying no harvest for the burs.
- A large bunch of grapes, then a large vat of grapes, came in the next scene.
- A great vat of grape juice was stirring around and a-round with no visible paddle moving it.
- Green bottles were being filled with grape juice or wine, but again with no visible hand doing this action.
- A beautiful, clear spring of water became muddy and silt-laden and then dried up entirely.
- The lovely, clear-violet light of God swept up and disappeared, then started low and swept up again and again many times, ending in heavenly lights and jewels.
- A dim light of no color drifted down and faded out to complete blackness. This same scene was repeated three times, ending in complete blackness. Then flames appeared in the middle of the blackness.
- A huge, green worm with an ugly, revolting head filled the entire screen. This was accompanied by the odor of evil that I have smelled once or twice – a foul smell like nothing I have been able to identify.
- A fat train moved relentlessly at a high rate of speed.
- A wide roadway kept getting wider.
- A man stood by an automobile with five or six children by him – some his and some were from another family.
- A woman turned and walked back alone.
- Fire appeared again, this time covering the entire screen. Accompanying that was the very bad odor of Satan.

I believe this is an accurate report of the sequence of pictures. It resembles the harvest in Revelation but is more detailed. I had absolutely no influence on the scenes. My mind was whirling fast to see and understand the pictures. As soon as I acknowledged one, it disappeared and the next appeared. It was about six in the morning, completely dark.

There can be no doubt that Revelation is truly the story of the end of time. There is a heaven and a hell and many people are doomed to destruction, darkness and flames. I think the Lord is telling me to act quickly to witness for Jesus in order to save some people from destruction.

John who wrote Revelation told what he saw in visions. His own theology or experience or knowledge of history had nothing to do with the visions, as implied by some commentaries.

March 2, 1988—

Rain started last evening but briefly let up this morning when we were deciding whether or not to stop by the Aransas National Wildlife Refuge on our way home. A rare crimson-collared grosbeak, a visiting songbird from Mexico, reportedly had been seen at a certain location on the refuge and we wanted to see it.

When we arrived in the vicinity, God sent a bright red cardinal to draw our attention to a particular bush, then placed the grosbeak next to the cardinal so we would see it. There is something about seeing a new species of bird that imparts a deep sense of satisfaction to a bird-watcher, even though in this case the new bird was female and very drab—the color of a dark leaf on a dark day.

We praised God for finding it for us and for delaying the rain. As we were leaving, two people drove up and asked about the grosbeak. I took them back to the area, pointed out the bush where we had seen it and told them what to look for. It was gone but I told them to hang around because I thought it might soon be back. I had barely gotten back into the car to leave when the rain started again and continued most of the day.

How wonderful it is to have the Lord so close, paying attention to the smallest detail of our lives, protecting, healing, loving, showing us his world, saving us from accident and making himself known so tenderly and lovingly.

March 5, 1988 –

Not long ago I conceived the notion that television itself might be the Antichrist. It is universal and evil in much of its content and influence, destroying family relationships, fostering immorality, illiteracy, violence, illicit sex and is degrading in many ways, besides robbing viewers of personal creativity.

But it is *not* the Antichrist. Last night the Lord sent a vision to straighten out my thinking. First came scenes of pink and blue fabrics, polka-dots, human-type designs and colors to illustrate the vision was to be of earth, not heaven. Then came an abstract vision showing two great, irregular balls of fog or spirit colliding to their destruction. Immediately to the side of this scene was the profile of a man with an Indian headdress—a chief. It was the middle of the night and my thinking was a little fuzzy. I thought, "Oh, the Lord is revealing an Indian conflict." Abruptly, the headdress on the man disappeared and I realized it had been sent to inform me he was a ruler, not an Indian chieftain, but an emperor, a dictator—the Antichrist. So a *person* will be the Antichrist, not a thing like television.

March 8, 1988 –

We met a couple from Minnesota at the K.O.A. in Waco, Texas. They own a small 40-acre farm, inherited from his parents, where he has lived all his life and they love it very much. A train derailment spilled heavy oil in the water supply, contaminating their spring, wells and the water table for miles, essentially ruining the farm, killing their animals and making them sick. They received compensation, but they really wanted their good farm back.

I prayed for the Lord to heal their land. They are innocent folks who are among the little people Jesus loved. As though in answer to my prayer, the Lord sent to my mind an obscure passage in Romans: *God ... who gives life to the dead and calls into existence the things that do not exist* (4:17). (Rejoicing, I set this message aside with plans to write and share it with them.)

March 12, 1988—

While in bed with my body resting and my spirit becoming quiet, I received from the Lord three visions: First, I saw the earth—actually, dirt and gravel with rain puddles around it. Immediately, the scene shifted to bright lights and the beautiful flashing jewels of heaven. In a moment I saw dirt again but not the same pattern as the first—this time, no puddles. Then came lights and jewels of heaven again. The third time the dirt formed itself into a road that traveled upward until it began to glow and light up with heavenly lights. This was all. I knew there was an explanation and it would surface shortly, so I stored the visions away and went to sleep.

This morning I awakened to the hymn "Rescue the Perishing, Pray for the Dying." I was obedient, praying fervently for those unknown persons who were dying.

I have asked the Lord several questions lately and have not received Scriptural answers that usually come from opening the Bible. Then it came to me that I had not acted on the answers given me in that manner during the recent past and the Lord is withholding answering until my priorities are straight.

The Lord sent a vision during the night of a fragment of a newspaper with a small round cutter beside it. The message is to glean carefully what I read. I must cut the evil side of worldly things unmercifully from my reading and consciousness.

March 14, 1988—

Today Nancy and I went to the hospital and prayed for two sick babies. One was an Infant Death Syndrome (I.D.S.) suspect whose mother told us he was turning blue at times when she laid him down. We asked her if we might pray for him and for her. She was so moved she cried when we prayed, sobbing out all her fears. We comforted her and told her to trust the Lord and that we'd return tomorrow. The other baby had pneumonia but was better. The Lord had been reminding me the last couple days that I should go to pray for sick babies.

While we were at the Rio Hondo campground in Texas, the Lord pointed out a man who was camping nearby and told me to give him the word of salvation. I thought of myriad reasons to postpone this: Howard was sick and I was busy, but the truth is, I just didn't do it. Since coming home, I have regretted it and asked forgiveness and worried about it. Then it came to me that I must send a letter, so here goes. I can mail it in care of the campground.

Dear Mr. Barnes,

My husband and I lived next door to you for a week in February. We didn't see you much because you were working and we were recovering from colds and flu. We are people who have strong faith in God and Jesus Christ and we want to tell you that your life is extremely valuable in God's sight. You are created in his image and he loves you for the very special person you are and desires that when your time on earth is finished, you spend eternity with him.

God's dwelling place is perfect justice and righteousness. Since none of us is perfectly righteous or just, God went to extreme measures to bring us into his presence and so sent a part of himself, a son—Jesus, to take our imperfections on himself and purify us by dying in our behalf. Death did not hold Jesus for God raised him up after he had been dead and sealed in a tomb for three days. His friends plus some 500 others saw him alive before he went back to God. Jesus made it possible for you and me to be forgiven and cleansed from our wrongdoing and imperfections – by simply calling on his name and accepting his gift of cleansing and forgiveness. But this must be more than lip service – it must be sincere.

The Lord is very interested in you because he has given me no rest until I should write to you about these things. You do not even need to take my word for it. If you will for one Sunday go down to the Rio Hondo Baptist Church and listen to the message of that fine minister of God, he will confirm what I have told you.

Our existence does not end at death; only the physical part ends. The soul or spirit of a person moves to another place which is determined by the One who created us. If we have chosen his way to live and have done our best and asked to be forgiven by the sacrifice of Jesus for the things we have done wrong, then we will live forever in the most beautiful place you can imagine – full of peace, love and joy. The alternative is unthinkable but, I'm afraid, very real – eternal darkness, loneliness, lostness, pain and emptiness.

There are people who care about you and God cares about you, else why would he go to such lengths to reach you with this message?

May the God of peace be with you, and may you live in his presence now and forever.

Sincerely,
D.G.

Though I had no concrete evidence, it was my feeling he had lost his way and was into things the Lord did not like. The Lord really wrote the above letter—it is his message. I mailed it immediately. [Mr. Barnes answered the letter with warmth and appreciation.]

March 15, 1988 –

Powerful waves of Spirit engulfed me last evening when I went to bed. Bells started ringing deep in my inner hearing. I felt this visitation was in response to my busy day yesterday working for the Lord.

He also is asking me to write to the Swensons [March 8 entry] whose farm was ruined and tell them this:

Dear Mr. & Mrs. Swenson,

You will be surprised to hear from me. We met in a Laundromat in Waco two weeks ago.

Your story of the poisoning of your family farm by a railroad accident has weighed heavily on my mind since then. We are Christian folks and I have prayed about this several times. The Lord has given me a special gift of being able to hear him at times. He places his message deep in my brain along with the knowledge that it is from him.

When I was praying about your situation, he said, quoting from Romans 4:17: *God ... who gives life to the dead and calls into existence the things that do not exist.* He left me with the understanding that the Lord, by a special work and act of his will, is cleansing your farm of its impurities. He can do that, you understand.

Since God created everything that is, he can dissolve everything that is. He raised Jesus from the dead—who had been sealed in a tomb for three days. His disciples and 500 other people saw Jesus alive again before he ascended into heaven and we celebrate this miracle every Easter.

Please look in the Bible at 2 Chronicles 7:14: *If my people who are called by my name will humble themselves, and pray and seek my face, and turn from their wicked ways, then I will hear from heaven, and will forgive their sin and heal their land.* So he did things like this even in Old Testament days.

If you are not now attending a Christian church in your area, I hope you will start. Declare your faith in God and his son Jesus, worship him and sing praises to him for his goodness and mercy to you and for healing your poisoned farm water supply. Taste the water and you will find it clean and pure. God created all of us and loves us enough to send his only son to take our sins, our pain and suffering and our accidents upon himself so that by believing we him might be healed and restored.

I hope your trip south was as much fun as ours. God bless you and keep you safe.

Sincerely,
D.G.

I just asked the Lord for a confirmation of the message in the letter to the Swensons and opened the hymnal by chance to "Hope of the World" by Georgia Harkness. "... God's gift from highest heaven, bringing to hungry souls the bread of life, still let thy Spirit unto us be given to *heal earth's wounds* and end her bitter strife."

Thank You, Father!!! I mailed the letter confident of its veracity.

[February, 1991—

I just telephoned the Swensons in Minnesota and they said they are living on the same farm, have drilled a new well, had the water tested and it is *good, pure water*. She also said they are going to church. *Praise God!]*

March 19, 1988—

Since I am very tired tonight, I asked the Lord for a hymn and he sent "Christ for the World We Sing" — "The world to Christ we bring; with loving zeal; the poor and them that mourn, *the faint and overborne,* sin-sick and sorrow worn, whom Christ doth heal."

As promised, I did return to the hospital to see about the little I.D.S. baby. He was much better and was to be released today. His mother was smiling and happy.

March 21, 1988—

At morning prayer Nancy spoke a message from the Lord and said, as closely as I can remember, "My children, I love you very much—much more even than you love your own children. I know your wants, your needs, your struggles. I am weeping now with you, but I want you to love me and praise me. Praise! Praise! That is all that is needed—for you to love me and praise me. If you only knew how much I can do for you if you give me your love and praise!" Amen, amen.

March 20, 1988 —

The Lord has been asking me to eat lighter and today the Bible opened to the first chapter of Daniel which tells of Daniel's refusal to eat the king's delicacies. It is a tough assignment, but I am trying.

March 24, 1988 —

Last week I had pains in the left shoulder blade area, a numb left arm, elevated blood pressure and difficulty breathing. I sought the Lord to heal me and he did. Two friends sensed my distress and were praying for me without my knowing.

Last evening right after retiring I experienced a wonderful communion with the Holy Spirit. As my eyes became accustomed to the dark, I began to see boiling clouds on the ceiling that looked like the underside of storm clouds in even lumps. In from the window started flowing red and white rays of light in thick bands that occasionally throbbed to the rhythm of the flickering flames of the Holy Spirit. It's hard to describe, but I saw flames around the darkened room, varying in intensity. Then the rhythm of the Spirit began to flow through me. I felt tingly and warm in my chest, abdomen and legs. This process continued for possibly an hour. I felt much at peace, loved, protected, cradled and, I'm sure, healed.

Jim Chauser [from my February 2, 1988 entry] called. He was so excited about going to Africa and around the world, he asked me to pray for his palpitating heart, which I will certainly do. Also I invited him to come see us. He never came. [We never heard from Jim again. His phone is disconnected.]

March 27, 1988—

At about first light this morning, something caused me to open my eyes. There were strange dots of light the size and shape of a person in front of me. Then I started seeing a face and became frightened. I told Miriam today, and she said chills ran up her spine.

Sometime near this date, the Lord said to me, "I will not let them go." I had been worrying about my unsaved friends and this message was to assure me of their eventual salvation. He also indicated I am to continue to pray for them.

March 28, 1988—

I ate lightly last night, hoping for a return of the angel. Much light and movement circulated around the room but there was no discernible form. At one time, the room appeared quite pebbly, with rainbow colors in each bubble or pebble. Once I felt the bed quiver with the rhythm of the Holy Spirit which swept over me internally from head to toe.

In the midst of this communion experience, I heard the Lord mention the number, 87. I asked what it meant, and this morning, the Bible opened in my hand to Psalm 34:11-14: *I will teach you the fear of the Lord. Which of you* **desires life, and covets many days to enjoy good?** *Keep your tongue from evil, and your lips from speaking deceit. Depart from evil, and do good; seek peace, and pursue it.* I receive this to mean the Lord is giving me 87 years to live if I myself do not shorten it by living and doing foolishly—or if the Lord Jesus doesn't come before then.

March 30, 1988 —

I was very sick last night. A tight band gripped my chest, I was feverish and couldn't inhale or exhale. My blood pressure soared and pulse rate was very high. The doctor had started antibiotics, but they hadn't taken effect yet, so pneumonia almost took my life before the morning light. I spent most of the night sitting in the kitchen over the vaporizer. All the while, God sent flashing lights and quivering flames of the Holy Spirit. Both the bed and my body quivered to the rhythm of the Holy Spirit. This morning, Howard took me to the doctor again and I am recovering rapidly. Praise God!

During the period when I was the sickest, the Lord sent his precious violet light into my eyes. Then while I was looking at it, a straight arrow came from above and penetrated the light. The arrow was composed of rainbow colors! I knew during the night that the number "87" the Lord gave me two days ago was to uphold my morale during this crisis. Also this illness brought to mind the visions I had [March 12 entry] of seeing an "earth to heaven" scene three times. It was my near death I was seeing—first from a possible heart attack two weeks ago, next the pneumonia that almost took me last night and a third event which will take place later. The vision of it was a road that slowly climbed upward to heaven.

March 31, 1988 —

The sound of angel's wings caught my consciousness this morning. There were four of them—a flutter, then a pause, then a flutter—four times. Immediately the song "Angels in Bright Raiment" came to mind so I would know the sound was of angels. I sat up in bed and received a message: "You will write several books for me!"

April 1, 1988 –

The Lord is healing me rapidly from the near pneumonia. It is Good Friday and I am listening to the Fauré "Requiem." God is very near. Since it is raining, I did not go to the worship services tonight, but Howard did. I am communing with the Lord at home.

So many revelations of God have come to me. In listening to tapes of Genesis, I discovered that Abraham experienced the presence of God in fire and cloud when he made a sacrifice: ... *a smoking fire pot and a flaming torch passed between these pieces* 15:17. Also, it occurred to me that the promise of God to Noah was a cloud with a rainbow in it.

April 3, 1988 –

Today is Easter Sunday. Hallelujah! He is risen!

Powerful events occurred here last night. The Lord nudged me awake and started sending waves of Spirit through me. I saw ripples of colored light sweep over me accompanied by the most comforting, warm sensations—love and peace and complete freedom from fear. This continued for two hours. Once I saw a small dot of color become first an emerald, then a ruby, an amethyst and a diamond before it faded. Also from time to time, the entire room lit up with the light of the Holy Spirit.

When I closed my eyes I was sent a vision of Satan—a fierce, helmeted, bearded warrior with a scowl of anger on his face and a mouth opened in anger and cruelty. Immediately, I repeated the name, "Jesus," several times. The vision disappeared completely.

Around four something awakened me. I began to anticipate some happening because I was surrounded by a pebbly light with dark lines surrounding each pebble. I knew I was in the

Spirit because there was an undercurrent of noise, no discernible sound, but a dim far-off roar. I felt extremely weak, as though I couldn't move because my body had been seized by something. I looked out the window, while still in bed, and saw *the largest person I have ever seen!* He also was a warrior and was standing in the back corner of the yard. It was a cloudy figure with a bright light behind him illuminating his outline and he appeared to have a helmet and be dressed for battle.

While I watched, the fog intensified, enlarged and brightened before my eyes as the light from behind accentuated the figure. I asked who it was and received the reply, *"Michael!"* I saw three other foggy figures around him who were all over seven feet tall. I asked if they had a message and was told they did, but that I will know the message when the time comes. Now they were protecting me from Satan, the one whom I had seen. I asked why Satan was after me, and they said I had been ordering him out of so many places, he was trying to get at me.

I remembered ordering Satan, in Jesus' name, from the town, from floods, storms, the government, the country, even the world. I am not afraid because the angels I saw certainly have more power than Satan. They are the army of Jesus.

I became excited and started getting more awake and out of the Spirit. As I did, the intensity of the figures dimmed but did not disappear. One has to be in the Spirit or look with spiritual eyes to see spiritual things.

The figures did not appear to move but they were real. The columns of fog represented angels and one day I will see them in detail and living color. I must not be ready for that yet. I was in tremendous awe but not afraid. I am still in awe!

It is hard to think of spiritual beings without a physical form. Do angels really have physical forms or do they manifest one in order that mortals may be able to see them?

A terrible cosmic conflict is taking place in the universe. If people only knew that when they choose sin and disobedience, they are choosing Satan and his cohorts.

April 4, 1988 –

Though I looked last night, I'm not certain the angels were there. The Lord is saying, "Yes, they were," but my eyes could not be certain. I am, however, continuing in Jesus' name to order Satan out of situations where evil seems to be present.

One thing certain last night was the color pink. The Lord sent a vision in which rows and rows of pink flowers made up the scene. Everything else seemed to be pink as well. The Lord said, "I give you a basket of flowers."

The Lord said to me this morning, "Pray and praise without ceasing!" So I prayed all day as I went about daily activities. I took my friend Delilah to Broken Arrow to attend Kenneth Hagin's healing seminar and am terribly tired tonight.

April 6, 1988 –

I must review the events of the past three days to explain what happened the night of April 4th. Saturday night, April 2, I saw the huge angels who said they were protecting me. On Monday morning, April 4, the Lord told me to pray without ceasing, which I did—but then I went to bed exhausted. Mighty waves of Spirit went though me that night as I prayed and praised. When I started to go to sleep, *a powerful explosion* almost knocked me out of bed. But it was in the spiritual realm and the only thing it did was render me wide awake.

I looked outside and thought I saw spirits in conflict. I prayed, "Jesus, Jesus, praise him, praise him," many times. An hour later I started to sleep again, and again was almost blasted out of bed. I started praying again and had the feeling Jesus was asking me to stay awake and watch with him. And pray. So I did, sometimes in tongues and sometimes in English.

One more time, around two, I started drifting off to sleep and again a powerful, thundering blast shook me awake. I continued praying until after four when peace seemed to settle around me and I went to sleep. Sometime after this Jesus woke me gently and planted a "Victory in Jesus," hymn in my mind and I knew he had conquered.

Sometime during the night, possibly after the first blast, I started seeing visions. There must have been at least three, but they made no sense. Jesus said these visions were closed and I was not to speak of them just as John of Patmos was ordered not to write about the message given him by the seven thunders. The next morning Jesus sent a lively song about sunshine, "Heavenly Sunshine" which I sang all day.

April 9, 1988 —

I ate lightly last night. At bedtime, the Holy Spirit was strongly present in the form of heat in my palms. I looked toward the window and started getting in the Spirit. I saw a foggy face with an expression of anger at the window. "Jesus, Jesus," I said and felt the embrace of the Holy Spirit. I ordered the evil spirit away in the name of Jesus several times and saw the features fade, but it did not completely disappear. Then a foggy arm encircled it from behind and everything faded. I asked God to post angels nearby for protection and went to sleep. *God help us!* What is happening in this world?

Several times lately the Lord has opened the Bible for me to the passages about Jesus' temptations by Satan. I think this was to warn me of these attacks. According to Miriam, someone in the Evangelism Committee warned of the same thing the other night, and they all prayed God's protection.

April 17, 1988 –

Delilah and I have just completed two weeks of Kenneth Hagin's healing school. The last day I was so tired I could hardly drive those 60 miles, but a most wonderful and unique resurrection took place. After the usual Bible lesson, we were instructed to start walking around the room singing praises to God for his healing and love, clapping our hands and skipping. Soon we were whirling and dancing in the Spirit while singing God's praises in an exuberant and enthusiastic acclaim of his goodness. Delilah was still wheelchair-bound, but she received the spirit energy along with the rest of us. I was so full of vigor, I drove home singing and praising God and did a half-day's work on arrival. Even at bedtime I was not sleepy.

In the middle of the night last week I heard the flutter of wings—small and delicate fluttering like a tiny cherub. I saw it in profile and the flutter of the wings was on the upper back as wings would be! *I was totally amazed!*

Last night I saw an angel posted in the backyard. A shadow in the shape of a person was surrounded by light. He was quite tall, moved slightly from time to time and seemed to be standing in the air some five feet off the ground. There were no wings. The legs were separated so it did not have a robe. One arm was free and moved. I asked who it was and am not certain of the answer, though he said he was protecting us.

April 20, 1988 –

Yesterday a hymn tune played in my head all day: "He is Lord" – "he is risen from the dead, and he is Lord. Every knee will bow, every tongue confess that Jesus Christ is Lord."

At the time I didn't know why it was sent but found out last night. We attended a worship service with a sermon by Kenneth Hagin and then fell into bed after eating very little. In the night I awakened to see a figure in the backyard—a shadow outlined with light which was elevated some three feet off the ground. I saw the hands rise to the head, then reach out to a small object of light the Lord said was a baby.

Somehow, into my mind was placed the knowledge that the figure was Jesus. In fact, he became very bright and changed colors from a creamy white to violet—the color of God or Jesus. The word "baby" came to me and the Lord said to my inner being, "You are to lay hands on Tim and Laura's baby and bless her." (That baby is not born yet, but the Lord is calling it a *her*.) Also he indicated we are to journey to Hawaii to do this. Hurray! What a wonderful opportunity! Tim is my nephew in the U.S. Navy, stationed in Hawaii.

In the same vein the Lord is asking me to give up all secular influences and stimuli and concern myself with him and his holiness alone so that I may be further sanctified for his service. Thank you, Father, for that honor.

April 21, 1988 —

Again last night I saw a figure in the backyard. I was in bed completely relaxed, looking out the low window. The venetian blind was half-way up and the curtains were drawn back. I recognized that I was in the Spirit by the way everything looked and the way I felt. The figure took on the appearance of a shepherd with a staff.

As soon as I acknowledged what it was, it shrank to half size and looked like a pregnant woman. I wondered who that represented, then it shrank further and looked like a baby. That must have been *Mary with the baby Jesus.* The baby grew and became young Jesus. Both of Jesus' hands were very bright, like light. I assume this represented the healing power in his hands.

After the figure Jesus grew to normal size, I saw a semi-circle of faces around him. Some of the faces became masks of horror and fell away into darkness.

Then I saw a large, black figure with two bright yellow eyes attack Jesus. It was the size of Jesus, but it fell away from him, came to my window and looked in. I ordered it away in the name of Jesus and it withdrew, but not far. I saw traces of that evil force the remainder of the time the story was progressing, but not at my window. These figures were foggy shapes resembling the characters in the story. *Jesus was showing his story right before my eyes!*

There was much movement of form and light, but alas no other piece of the story registered. Then I saw a huge cross superimposed over the Christ-figure. I prayed. When the cross disappeared, I saw the figure of Jesus take on brightness and color with tiny rays of light radiating out from him in a full circle—that represented the Resurrection. During the Resurrection scene, everything took on a lovely blue color. The story was over, but I was ready to leap out into the yard and dance around five feet off the ground for sheer joy!

April 22, 1988 –

I awakened in the night to someone breathing beside me, though Howard was in another room. I heard heavy breathing and thought it was my own breathing at first, so I held my breath and listened. The breathing continued. I sat up in bed and looked around. Nothing! The sound stopped. Then I understood and laughed because the Holy Spirit was teasing me.

I told this to Miriam today and she gasped, because *the same thing happened to her last night.* Amazing!

April 23, 1988 –

On reading Acts 2 and 3—Peter's sermon where 3,000, then 5,000 people were converted, I realized there was something much more than Peter's words that would turn Jews of long heritage in another direction. It had to be the power of the Holy Spirit in the Pentecost event and in the hearts of the people. We still have that power available, sent from God and in Jesus' name.

It is all in the Bible: complete truth, total wisdom, every principle—everything needed for all generations in all times is there in *The Word.* God knew this was a way to spread truth from generation to generation and has power to cause things to be written or not written, accepted as canon or not accepted, copied correctly down through the ages or discarded in the copying if not of God. He saw that this *Word* was to be called *his Word,* so one must be careful in accepting just any translation of that *Word.* It would be good to be able to read the original Greek and Hebrew.

April 25, 1988 –

Last night I saw a representation of myself outside just where I have been seeing others. At first, I didn't know who it was. A foggy image of a tiny child appeared, then grew. A Spirit stood above and to the right of it, and from the Spirit straight lines of light descended to the figure. This must have been the blessing of the Holy Spirit watching over and protecting the person growing up. Then the head and left hand of the figure lit up, and I knew who was being represented. After a while the Holy Spirit seemed to come down beside me.

While I was growing up, in the fog image, a sweet gum tree behind the image started weaving back and forth in the wind. The figure moved back and forth with it, representing, I imagine, the instability of my youth. Toward the end of the picture series the tree started weaving again, but the figure stood still. Then the Lord told me it was I. All at once, he brightened the fog and lighted it with blue light.

I felt the Lord's touch on my lip today. It was like a mild electric shock.

April 26, 1988 –

In the night I saw an image of Jesus with a crown on. I was beside him and *he was holding my hand.* His figure lit up with light and color. My image shone dimly, as though a reflection of his glory. Later in the same place I saw a large black image with two brilliant yellow eyes. I ordered it away in the name of Jesus. How grateful I am for God's angel protection.

April 27, 1988 –

When I discussed the war between Satan and God's angels that I saw a few days ago with others in the church, they told me they had detected a similar attack by Satan. Revelation 12:7-12 speaks of a battle where Satan is cast out of heaven and is angry because he has such a short time left. I am seeing more evil spirits lately, or is it that I am more able to perceive them?

April 28, 1988 –

Last night I saw some spirits in the backyard. They were dark so I suspected evil. One appeared to have a large cat head with evil yellow eyes. I ordered them away in the name of Jesus and they all departed. This morning I woke to the Lord saying, "Stay until I send the Holy Spirit upon you"—from

Luke 24:49. Since I am having trouble with my eyes when out in the bright sunlight, I suspect this message concerns them.

May 1, 1988 —

I awakened at four this morning and saw bright lights in the backyard in the shape of a figure. The lights were white, then red, green, gold and violet. I knew it had to be a powerful angel, perhaps Michael. The expression on his face was fierce; he was about eight feet tall, standing some five feet in the air.

May 4, 1988 —

Two days after the Lord told me to wait on the Holy Spirit to heal my eyes, I felt an extraordinary wave of Spirit pass through me. This lasted a long time and the next morning, Sunday, the large floaters in my eyes had disappeared.

Satan has been attacking us lately. A brown recluse spider was suspended over the bed by a single strand from the ceiling light. I killed it. A coyote ran across the highway near the county line, and our car missed it by a hair. We were driving the little Toyota and might have overturned if we had hit it. A new carpet we ordered was miscut, sent across the country and then had to be returned.

I repudiated Satan and all his work, binding him in the name of Jesus, casting him into outer darkness. "Lord," I said, "please fill all my space with thy precious Holy Spirit. Thank you, Jesus." I saw many spirits standing around our backyard last night and asked Jesus about this. I received a tune in my mind, "We are standing on holy ground ... and I know that there are angels all around ..." They appeared as white columns of fog with misty faces and they were standing off the ground.

The Lord told me today a message was coming. I opened the Bible twice to the book of Samuel.

May 17, 1988—

I didn't eat much last night. It is easier to see into the spirit world when one's stomach is not busy. I sat in a chair praying, wishing I could hear the Lord talk back to me, so when I went to bed, he started flashing pictures on my west window. First appeared a string of stylized animals: cattle, camels and elephants. I immediately thought, "Oh, the Lord is going to play Noah before me." The next scene consisted of people moving from right to left across the lower window. These seemed to represent the world population as they were stiff, stylized and without features. Then came an image of Noah with both hands raised above his head.

After a time I saw the sea—huge waves with a casket-like box floating on them. The sea covered the place where the people had been. Then the ark floated across the screen and disappeared. All these scenes took a long time and I went to sleep before anything else took place. One thing is certain— whatever the Lord plays for me is true. There was a Noah, an ark and a flood.

May 21, 1988—

How beautiful it is here at Rock Creek State Park with the warblers and thrushes singing and wild flowers coming into bloom. We just returned from hiking the mountain and taking pictures of wild flowers. The Lord kept showing us a straggly white one which I said wasn't pretty enough to photograph, but he made us stop to examine it. Through six-power magnification it showed little white spirals with orchid-colored polka-dots—magnificent!

Yesterday I hiked up the warbler road from the camping area to beyond the park boundary. From time to time I waded through tall grass and brush to locate warblers off the trail. I prayed and praised and talked to the Lord the entire time and came out without a tick or chigger or mosquito bite.

As I was walking back, the Lord called my attention to a scarlet tanager near the top of a tall ash tree. I have never seen a more beautiful bird—with its scarlet body, black wings and tail—perched in a leafy tree against the deep cerulean sky. Not even the same scene in heaven could be more beautiful.

Tim and Laura's baby was born yesterday. It is an eight-pound, seven-ounce little *girl* named Julia. This is the one the Lord told us to lay hands on and ask his blessing.

May 22, 1988–

I am becoming more aware not only of God's interest in every detail of our lives but also in actually planning those details. When we are operating within his will, we are following the details he has already worked out for our best good as well as that of everyone else. When we do not follow his will, we fall into nature's vast happenstance or chance and become heir to anything Satan can offer against us. It is astonishing to think that God plans everything so thoroughly.

May 26, 1988–

Last night I saw a shape I couldn't identify at the window. There was much movement and activity in the room and cloud lumps covered the ceiling so I asked what was going on. A tune came to mind: "I looked over Jordan, and what did I see; a band of angels coming after me; coming for to carry me home. Swing low, sweet chariot, coming for to carry me home ... " So the crowd was a band of angels and the shape I saw was a chariot. Amazing!

Sometime during this program I saw the shape of an angel

wing accompanied by the foggy silhouette of the angel. But the wing was distinct and bright. It was a light-green color and looked transparent, sort of gossamer—thin and delicately ribbed. Also I saw whirling wheels on the chariot. I wonder what this means?

June 1, 1988 –

I returned from Missouri yesterday. Betty rode part of the way with me and we asked God to station angels around us for protection. As we traveled, she commented that every car passing us going in any direction was white. It was that way for many miles. God showed me he sent them to symbolize the angels who were protecting us. How good the Lord is!

June 4, 1988 –

The Lord inserted the words "new name" into my consciousness last night. I asked what this meant and meditated on it. Then the word *Samuel* came to mind. Samuel means "name of God" and Samuel carried the message to Eli the priest about the abominations of his sons.

June 7, 1988 –

Nancy received a message from the Lord last week and gave a copy to everyone in the Monday Prayer group. It is a letter from the Lord and is so comforting.

O, my children,
When trials come, whether large or small, *know* these also are for your good. Exercise your faith, just as one exercises one's muscles to strengthen them. Count it *all* blessings, my loved ones. Be not therefore anxious as concerning *anything* that touches you, for my care for you is constant, as certain as the sun and moon that shine even when they are so obscured by clouds their light seems dimmed on earth.

Trials may be used for *my* purposes, both in those who are directly affected and in those who are concerned for the one immediately affected. Your compassionate love, evidenced in your prayers, is sweet fragrance to me.

I hold each of you in my arms, as a mother holds her precious babe. I hold each of your hands, as a father holds the hand of his toddler learning to walk. I stand at the end of the track as each of you runs the special race for which you have been entered. The prize is not a medal, nor glory, but strength increased, endurance gained – spiritual muscle built.

Your faith is a delight to me. It has the fragrance of sweet incense to me. Your heartfelt concern for others in their trials is but a shadow of my concern for them – and for *you.* Truly *I am in you and with you* in all things and all times. Fear not for I am your God and nothing shall touch you that is not within my will for you. All things truly do work together for *your good.*

Each of you has a special place in my plan. Each of you serves a special *purpose.* I treasure your closeness to me, your openness to my direction, your willingness to be "different" – even to be thought a bit "odd" for my sake. Be bold. Step out in faith. Know that I am with you at all times.

Do not be discouraged nor dismayed when things do not *seem* to be working in accordance with your prayers. See my will in all things, and know that *I am your God – your all in all!*

June 11, 1988 –

Last night after retiring, when my spirit quieted and my eyes adjusted to the dark, I saw great waves of Spirit roll in the window—not exactly colors, but as though a river of light and Spirit surged toward me. It was very strange. Whatever it was bent the light waves so the window narrowed in my vision. The Spirit river became a lens which distorted the outline of the window. At one time I saw a great wheel with spokes whirling in the middle of the Spirit river.

June 13, 1988—

We just returned from Springfield where my brother Basil had open-heart surgery. He is still in serious condition and we await better news by morning. The whole family gathered for mutual comfort.

In the recovery room we were allowed to see him and I touched him, praying for his life. I heard the Lord say he would live. My Bible opened to a passage in the Gospel of John, and my eye fell on the words: "he will not die." Praise God! We prayed all the way home. Our church and all our friends prayed, also Basil's church and Betty's church.

What wonderful memories I have of Basil. He is ten years my senior so was half-grown when Betty came along. I was born two years later and he thought the house was very full of girls—but he was good to us anyway.

I remember his racing down the blacktop road to me when I fell and broke an arm while walking to school. When I saw my distorted forearm I started screaming. The next thing I knew, I was in his arms being carried back up the hill.

I'll never forget the day our parrot flew away. I was totally distraught because I had taken him out of the cage and outdoors for a look at the world when he up and flew off. Never, I thought, would I see him again. But Basil saw him in a hickory tree down in the pasture, climbed the tree, and captured him. The parrot was as happy to be back as I was to have him.

Basil always gave us the nicest gifts. The Christmas I was eight, he gave Betty and me a single-shot Daisy BB gun each. What hours of pleasure we had hunting in the fields and woodlands of our farm. We never shot at anything alive except in our imagination and the only real trouble it got me in was when I shot a tiny hole through the kitchen window.

To us Basil always seemed so grown-up. He fixed our swings, built a tree platform for us, treated when he had money, teased at every opportunity and drove us on errands when he got his driver's license, or maybe even before. We loved him fiercely.

Dressing this morning to go to Springfield, I pulled on my panty hose and poked a finger right through them at the waist. A runner formed that went the length of the panty section and four inches into the stocking. I kept them on and went on my way. Sometime during the day, the Lord reknit all of the runner except the top hole I made with my finger. (I interpreted this to mean the Lord was planning to reknit Basil partially.)

June 15, 1988 –

We received bad news about Basil today: he has a hole in his lung, is paralyzed on one side, swollen and in dangerous condition. I was upset and depressed all day; however while taking a shower, I seemed to get a message from the Lord. He is giving Basil another chance and he will live and be have an opportunity to know God before dying.

Also deep in my spirit I realized that whatever happens is OK. I will be granted strength and courage to face anything. This message was planted so lovingly and tenderly in my mind and accompanied by such a feeling of peace that I knew it was from the Lord. I haven't worried about Basil since.

June 16, 1988 –

Good news! Praise the Lord! There is no hole in Basil's lung and he lifted his so-called paralyzed arm. He is going to be all right, just as the Lord said. He is partially conscious and breathing on his own. I am praising the Lord and thanking him for the healing. How good the Lord is!

Two nights ago, I awakened to see a transparent spirit beside the bed. I could make out an outline of a tall person but no features. It disappeared immediately.

We are starting into another drought this summer. In 2 Samuel when there was a drought and famine, David asked God how they had sinned. When the sin was discovered and atoned, the rains came.

I plan to ask the Lord about the drought. Also concerning the seven bowls of the wrath of God in Revelation, the sixth bowl causes the drying up of a great river. I noticed in today's paper that the Mississippi River is drier in some places than ever recorded.

June 17, 1988–

Today I went with the United Methodist Women to Andersonville to a District Day Apart. After lunch I was sitting in the back of the sanctuary about to go to sleep when I heard the soloist sing the words, "What I have promised, I will do." This came in so clearly to me, I snapped awake. God was telling me he is fulfilling his Word about healing Basil. Praise him!

The Lord keeps sending the hymn "I've Found a Friend" – "He loved me ere I knew him; he drew me with the chords of love, and thus he bound me to him; and round my heart still closely twine those ties which naught can sever, for I am his and he is mine, forever and forever."

June 20, 1988–

Last night worship was glorious. Pastor Charlie told us to be at peace and silent to allow God to speak to us. During the night God sent a beautiful, clear-violet light to my window. It kept getting more and more intense until I wondered if I would be swallowed up by this glory. A wheel was whirling beside it

and within the wheel flashed fire. I felt the supreme embrace of
the Holy Spirit and the whole bed shook to the rhythm of the
flickering flames of the Spirit. I lay awake until after midnight.

June 21, 1988 –

We went to see Basil today and returned this evening. I
thought he responded somewhat to me, but couldn't be sure.
He was semi-conscious. I laid my hands on him (head and
hand) and prayed. The atmosphere in the room was not condu-
cive to prayer but I did my best. Betty thinks he is near death
and I allowed myself to doubt his healing.

In the midst of the anguish of my own sin—doubting God's
repeated word to me—I felt something touch my lips. It was as
though a small electric shock grazed both lips. It stung a little—
prickled, so to speak.

I felt the presence of the Holy Spirit all night. I asked forgiveness of the Lord and felt as though I finally knew the depth
of my sin. I understood the meaning of Joshua standing before
God in filthy robes (Zech 3:3). My robes are filthy also and I
can—and did sin—exceedingly. But the Lord took me back
almost before I asked. Bless him.

Satan is insidious and clever, ever alert to find the one crack
in our armor. If we slip in any way, he is there to make a fool
of us and inflict damage.

I notice on reading 2 Chronicles 7:13-14 that people must
repent and turn to God for the promise of rain and the healing
of the land. I am praying for rain—but one isn't enough. The
whole country must repent.

July 6, 1988 –

I just discovered a fascinating passage in Daniel 7:9-14: *As I
watched, thrones were set in place, and an Ancient One took his*

throne, his clothing was white as snow, and the hair of his head like pure wool; his throne was fiery flames, and its wheels were burning fire. A stream of fire issued and flowed out from his presence. A thousand thousands served him, and ten thousand times ten thousand stood attending him. The court sat in judgment, and the books were opened. ... As I watched in the night visions, I saw **one like a human being coming with the clouds of heaven.** *And he came to the Ancient One and was presented before him. To him was given dominion and glory and kingship, that all peoples, nations and languages should serve him. His dominion is an everlasting dominion that shall not pass away, and his kingship is one that shall not be destroyed.*

Amen. I am seeing snatches of things Daniel saw long ago.

July 11, 1988 –

The Lord sent the hymn "There Shall be Showers of Blessings" today. Sure enough, it has been a blessed day including rain which was sorely needed.

July 16, 1988 –

The Lord told me he was preparing my way for driving to Springfield alone as Howard couldn't go that day. I did go and the drive was easy—no problems at all. I laid hands on Basil and prayed for continued healing. The visit with the rest of the family was good.

July 19, 1988 –

Last night the Lord showed me a quilt held together by a purple foundation. He encircles, supports, frames, outlines, highlights and unifies all life. Praise him!

Seldom have I felt so abandoned by everyone but the Lord. Howard was angry; Betty spoke sharply to me last week;

Miriam was rather cool; Carolyn, my bird-watching buddy, didn't seem to care; Fran insulted me; I even thought for a time that the Lord had cooled off toward me. But I know he still loves me and carries me in the palm of his hand. As it turned out the attack was of the evil one, and as soon as I figured it out, everything and everyone straightened out.

July 22, 1988 —

Today I visited Basil in Springfield. He is much better and starting to move his paralyzed leg. He is alert, knows what is going on, can sit alone and rise from his wheelchair. He still cannot speak much. I thank God for healing Basil when he was so ill everyone thought he would die.

August 4, 1988 —

I just finished reading *Missiles Over Cuba* by Tom White. He told of dropping plastic-coated Scriptures in Spanish while flying near Cuba, then being forced to land and becoming a prisoner. Though tortured, he and other Christians were sustained in prison by the Lord. How much some people have suffered in behalf of Christ. One man in prison was very devout, helping the weaker and sicker prisoners, acting as a servant to them by washing their clothes by hand in a basin.

Last night I saw a vision of two figures holding a small baby or child between them. This must be Julia, the baby of my nephew Tim and his wife Laura. We have the honor of being asked to be her godparents and are going to Hawaii for the christening.

August 9, 1988 —

We are in Honolulu at the Mirimar Hotel on the 18th floor. From our balcony, or "lanai," we can see much of Waikiki, part of the Pacific Ocean and the mountains above Honolulu. It is a beautiful city without smog. I sat on the lanai this morning, watching the day break from first light to sunup. It was magic.

As I prayed and thanked God for keeping us safe on the plane trip, the scene took on sparkle and brilliance beyond belief. At the same time the Lord sent a Communion hymn. Then I started scanning the hotels around me with binoculars and saw a man draped only in a towel. I dwelt on that scene too long and when I took the glass down, the scene had become ordinary and lost its magic and sparkle. A momentary curious attitude had spoiled my sanctification.

On the plane coming over we met a young couple who were to be married in Honolulu. At the end of the journey I gave them my pocket New Testament as a wedding present.

August 13, 1988 –

The Lord sent many hymns of comfort and assurance this week. As I held Julia in my hands, I asked the Lord's blessing on her. We had dinner with the whole family at Tim's house— a wonderful visit with all.

The Lord has been with us so lovingly this week. When we have needed a parking place in the shade, one has appeared; when we went to the zoo to see tropical birds, the Lord brought them to the front of the cage; he protected our gear in the car, smoothed rough spots, saw that we obtained a good rental car and helped us find our way with no accidents, and no discomfort from traveling. Praise him!

August 16, 1988 –

The christening went well. Howard and I promised to help with Julia's religious training. Everyone wore leis and went to

Tim's house afterward for a reception. I had another opportunity to lay hands on Julia and pray.

The Lord wanted me to witness for him to my family while there and made this clear by sending the hymn, "Peal Out the Watchword," to my consciousness the night before we saw them. Somehow I couldn't or didn't do it. He was disappointed in me and opened the Bible to Matthew 9:37, *"The harvest is plentiful, but the laborers are few."* It is harder to witness to people you know than to strangers.

August 18, 1988—

Last night I slept fitfully until one or two because of the jet lag. Since I was restless, I asked the Lord to send an angel or something. I went to sleep again and woke in a short time seeing in a vision the face of an old, old man, heavily bearded with long, gray hair. His gray eyes were the only discernible feature on his head. The face then faded and I said to myself, "Why, he looked as old as ... " Then the word, *"Methuselah,"* came rushing to mind! I knew the Lord had put it there. I'm sure he was showing me Methuselah of the Bible, the oldest recorded living person—969 years old when he died.

So the stories of the ancient patriarchs are true—they were real—and very old! If Methuselah was real, so were Adam and Eve, Cain and Abel; the Garden of Eden was an actual place and Biblical accounts of the beginnings of our race are factual!

August 27, 1988—

The Lord caught my attention to Luke 9:62: *Jesus said to him, "No one who puts a hand to the plow and looks back is fit for the kingdom of God."* I wondered what I had done, but it was what I was going to do. I should have taken the warning. Later today I found myself scanning the seamy headlines in the supermarket tabloids while waiting at the checkout counter. That, I realized later, was an activity to avoid from now on.

August 29, 1988 –

After repeated urging by the Lord, I drove to the city to see Gary. He was lying curled up under a sheet; even his head was under something. While kneeling and praying at his bedside I saw and felt the flicker of the Holy Spirit so I knew God was present. He seems to be telling me today Gary is not in pain.

September 9, 1988 –

In the night I saw a silhouette of the evil one with horns and bright eyes at the window. Immediately I started praising God and it disappeared. Then wave after wave of Spirit covered me and I felt my feet and legs become hot.

Remembering the day's news, I ordered the evil out of the fires at Yellowstone Park, the floods in Bangladesh and the strife in South Africa.

Then it seemed the Lord said to me, "I am putting out the fires," adding, "There is much evil in the world because people sin against me." He continued, *"The end is near."*

I said, "The end cannot be very near because the Antichrist has not come."

He answered, "The Antichrist is already here!"

Wow! What am I hearing?

September 10, 1988 –

I am now receiving the joy that the Lord has been sending. Much of the summer was stressful and I had lost my joy. But the Lord has restored peace and joy in my heart and I feel his Spirit flooding my being.

The Lord has let me know that I do not always do his will

immediately and he cannot complete his plans unless I do. Most of the time I jump to do what he asks but when it comes to witnessing to nonbelievers, sometimes I stumble. I do it better by letter.

Last night before I went to sleep the Lord started sending scenes of beauty: a lovely wallpaper design, a brass scrollwork, a golden shield with a design and a specially patterned wall. This morning I realized he was sending this gift of fragments of heaven in response to my telling the patients at Heritage Manor Nursing Home to think only of good, pretty, positive things.

September 15, 1988—

Several times lately, I have awakened to hear the delicate flutter of wings next to my ear. Yesterday there was also a high-pitched chatter along with the flutter. No doubt cherubim were nearby.

September 18, 1988—

The Yellowstone fires are being put out with rain and snow. The Lord also dissipated the fury of Hurricane Gilbert before it reached the United States. However it did damage Jamaica, Cancun and other areas of Mexico.

We received over four inches of gently falling rain over about four days. On the night of the bad thunderstorms, God sent a vision of crosshatching across my window, indicating he would protect us and our house from the lightning storm.

September 28, 1988—

I had a vivid dream of our beloved, deceased minister George Beeman returning to preach at the old church. He came up to me and said, "I have kept track of your parents."

This was so unusual I knew it must mean he has seen them

in heaven. He drew very near to me when he talked and I saw those dark penetrating eyes that I remember so well.

October 14, 1988 –

Something completely different and wonderful happened last night. I listened to tapes of Psalms, prayed and worshipped before turning out the light. While kneeling at the bedside I was circled by a *red light* about six feet in diameter.

It was very red—like blood but it did not flicker like the flames of the Holy Spirit I am accustomed to seeing. Perhaps I was being symbolically bathed in the blood of Christ. Needless to say, I prayed and praised and wept at this honor. Once I looked up and there was no spotlight. I looked down and the light was there again. After a minute or so it faded out. I do remember eating very lightly at dinner.

After going to bed, I saw light coming in the window in thin lines. At one point I saw hands and arms in a prayerful position on the window blind and a chair or throne sitting opposite. The arms and hands were quite vivid. Then I began to see faces about the throne—many, many faces. In an instant they were gone and darkness enclosed everything.

October 20, 1988 –

I am praying for the whales that are trapped by ice near Barrow, Alaska. In prayer I covered the whole complex operation with the blood of Christ by the power of God.

This morning God sent a hymn, "There is Power in the Blood," to say he approves of my prayer. The east wind has opened a crack in the ice to within three miles of them and the army is furnishing an ice breaker to help. Also the Russians are bringing an ice breaker. The whole world has united in concern for the whales. The Lord said to me, "I am saving the whales."

I was so joyful this morning I wanted to sing and dance.

October 21, 1988 –

I have been thinking about the whales quite a bit lately, wondering about God's relationship with them. Waking from a nap I heard the Lord say, *"I came that they may have life, and have it abundantly"* (Jn 10:10). *They!* So God loves the whales too—and all the animals he has created.

That is why it so important that the slaughter of all living things be done with reverence, like kosher killing—humanely, and with prayer. That is also one of the reasons we live in sin and are in need of forgiveness for we participate in the inhumanity of stockyard killings whenever we eat what has been inhumanely slaughtered or carelessly and cruelly grown. All living things are the property of the Lord and are due respect.

Tonight we are camped in Rock Creek Park with the Methodist campers. Sylvia made stew everyone contributed to; several families ate together as we laughed and visited while the children rode bicycles around a circular path. Afterward while I was walking, the Lord sent a Communion hymn, "The bread is always consecrated that men divide with men."

October 22, 1988 –

Yellow Rock Trail was lovely and warm, even in late October, and I enjoyed the walk very much. The sky was pure and fresh and framed the autumn leaves in living pictures.

While strolling, I thought about last night. It was very dark so I assumed I would not be able to see God's color panorama that I see almost every night at home, but sometime in the middle of the night I partially awakened to see a strong violet light come toward me. As it neared, it slowed down and slowly crept to my pillow—then to the corner of my eye where it became a bright light, but I did not feel the embrace. After a while I saw a green light and felt the embrace when it came. I see these lights with eyes open or closed. My eyes, that were swimming with large floaters, have cleared up now. Praise God!

October 23, 1988 –

While walking near the park river, I smelled the stench of evil that I have experienced before. I prayed for the blood of Jesus to cover the park—everything and everyone in it—and systematically prayed for the entire world, ordering evil out in the name of Jesus, covering the globe with the blood of Christ. The stench disappeared immediately.

Then I realized what a powerful tool we have—the whole of Christendom has—to rid the world of evil and allow the Kingdom of God to return to the planet. This is what Jesus meant when he said, *"The kingdom of God has come near"* (Mk 1:15). He meant it was again accessible to the whole world. All we have to do is believe it and use that power. When Jesus said, *"The kingdom of God is within you"* (Lk 17:21) he meant that the kingdom is within our power by calling upon him and his blood. It is an awesome power, a holy power, an undefeatable power, an immeasurable power and God has given it to us by using the name of Jesus. Wow!!

October 29, 1988 –

We are home again. Yesterday after I walked up the mountain behind our house, the Lord was sad. I didn't know the extent of my sin until today when I realized that the little stray dog I yelled at was a test of my compassion. It was following me and I saw no way to take it or keep it. But I had verbally abused one of God's creatures after praying so hard for him to rescue the whales. Forgive me, Lord.

October 30, 1988 —

A very strange thing happened in the night. I am still digesting it, trying to analyze it. I opened my eyes in the middle of the dark night and looked out into the backyard where it appeared to be *full daylight* with beautiful green grass, a brightly colored bird-bath and red and yellow flowers in places where there were no flowers. While watching in open-mouthed wonder, the night scene started rolling down over it like a window blind being drawn down from top to bottom—all very mysterious. The scene I was seeing must have been the spiritual equivalent of my physical universe. I am learning so much.

November 5, 1988 —

Though the wind was fierce this morning, I needed to go for a walk and think, but the strangest thing happened. The Lord sent angels to soften the wind before it hit me. It seemed odd to see limbs on trees bending deeply in the wind, yet feel very little on me. Even the roar of the wind sounded fierce. God is teaching me so much about his care.

November 6, 1988 —

The Lord sent an explanation of the windscreen last night in a vision of a foggy person with a shield in front of him. Bright arrows flew toward the shield but could not penetrate it. At the same time the Holy Spirit reminded me of the passage in Ephesians 6:16, *With all of these, take the shield of faith, with which you will be able to quench all the flaming arrows of the evil one.* So he not only protects us mentally and spiritually, but also physically in every way.

More than once when I have knelt to pray before retiring, the Lord has sent a circle of reddish light to cover me.

November 15, 1988—

At night I now tilt the blinds so the backyard is visible. Recently I saw a series of lines across my window in a 45° slope. While wondering about this, I saw a black blob with bright yellow eyes in the top of our sweet gum tree. How could an evil spirit be in the backyard? I regularly ask for the blood of Jesus to cover all our property. Immediately I ordered out all evil in the name of Jesus and closed the blind.

Later in the midst of the violet light sweeping over me, I asked to see the face of an angel or Jesus and the Lord sent a vision of the Turin cloth image of Jesus—a face with dark eyes, a long nose and the gaunt features of a tortured face.

November 18, 1988—

My lips are trembling often. Many storms have struck lately and I have asked the Lord to protect people from them. The trembling lips may have indicated that prayer was needed in advance of the storms. John & Paula Sanford, *The Elijah Task,* say sometimes prayer is not started soon enough or kept up sincerely enough to avert natural tragedies.

November 21, 1988—

The Lord told me he is keeping green leaves on our sweet gum tree until Christmas to show his care of us. Praise him! We've had a couple hard freezes and a two-inch snow, but its leaves are still green and alive. Tonight as I came in from examining it the Lord sent a hymn, "Great is Thy Faithfulness" by Thomas O. Chisholm – "Summer and winter, springtime and harvest; sun, moon and stars in their courses above join with all nature in manifold witness to thy great faithfulness, mercy and love."

November 24, 1988 –

The Lord has been warning me about the evil one coming in the window at night. I have been seeing evil faces through the opened venetian blind when I forget to close it. Last night I saw the head of a huge, horrible reptile—like an alligator or a dragon—with *fire coming out of its mouth* in a stream about three feet long.

Shuddering, I closed the window and blind and in the name of Jesus ordered the evil away from the house, the yard and the city. One has to be in the spirit or looking with spiritual eyes to see these things. If more people could see these evil monsters they are unleashing when they do evil or think about evil or talk of evil, it would stop in a hurry.

November 26, 1988 –

What a nice birthday! Howard gave me a topaz necklace and took me to dinner in the city. The Lord sent light and an angel into the bedroom shortly after we retired. Great rolls of light and color fogged in and I saw a huge blob of fog beside the bed—light amber in color and indefinite. I felt the presence as electricity through my body and praised God. Then the fog brightened brightly before it faded away in a few seconds.

November 29, 1988 –

Today something happened that is so wild and unbelievable I still tremble when I think about it. I saw a person whose face was familiar and who smiled and nodded to me. He was dressed in a suit, looked about 30 years of age and was playing catch-football with a boy.

I had awakened from an afternoon nap humming the tune, "Sweet Hour of Prayer." It was a reminder to go to the church to pray. While cruising Jefferson Street toward downtown, I noticed a man standing in the middle of my driving lane about a block away. He was glancing at me from time to time, but his main attention was focused on a small boy with whom he was playing catch-football. The boy remained on a side street, out of the way of traffic—but there was no traffic and no moving vehicle on either street, except mine.

I started slowing down, but while continuing to close in on them I noticed the man still standing where he was, in the middle of my driving lane. That's odd, I thought. Why doesn't he move to the curb? By this time my car was traveling very slowly and he was only a few feet away. Just then the football got away and rolled across the street. I almost stopped in case the boy ran after it, but he didn't. The man stepped aside, to the right side of my car, but not before he leaned over my windshield, looked directly into my eyes, smiled and partially nodded. In the process I looked at his face. It was the kindest, most loving face I have ever seen.

Rolling on slowly I thought, this man must be a minister of God and I knew I had seen him before. I started reviewing the places I had seen ministers but couldn't put a finger on his identity. He had dark hair, a dark suit, dark eyes with striking features and wasn't quite six feet tall. The purity and love on that face still shakes me. Why did I drive on?

When I came home and picked up the Turin portrait, I knew who he was. I asked for confirmation and the Bible opened to Acts and the disciples' experience with the resurrected Christ. This visitation is mentioned in John 14:21, *"They who have my commandments and keep them are those who love me; and those who love me will be loved by my Father, and I will love them and **reveal myself to them**."*

I am stunned and in shock over this event. I know I am not

to tell this right now, but it is hard to keep from running up and down the street yelling the news and dancing for joy.

December 5, 1988—

What shall I do with this good news? Jesus is alive and walking around on earth from time to time, revealing himself to people on occasion! Was it a vision? Perhaps, but he looked solid! He went to heaven in the flesh, so he still has flesh. In any case I don't have to know. It is enough to visualize this miracle with my own eyes! It is something no one can take away—a memory that will sustain me forever!

December 10, 1988—

I'm not certain my feet are tracking in a straight line after the above event but other things are happening that I must report. This morning the Lord sent the message, *A thousand may fall at your side, ten thousand at your right hand, but it will not come near you* (Ps 91:7).

I awakened yesterday morning to the vision of a vertical rainbow on the window blind. When I complained that I had not heard the fluttering of cherubim wings lately, the Lord sent fluttering just as I awakened this morning. Praise him!

Since seeing the dragon with fire, I have kept the window and blind closed at night. Also I distinctly heard the Lord say, "Close the window."

December 19, 1988—

Today we agreed to a price for the house of our dreams with an exquisite view of the valley and rolling hills beyond. It is a beautiful brick house with a two-car garage, a nice den overlooking the valley, a deck, a large lawn, three bedrooms and all electric. It is a very tight house—no cracks, no obvious flaws. Howard loves it as much as I.

The Lord must have heard my inner yearnings for a place to live with a good view. It is no coincidence that every day when I walked up this mountain for the sake of my heart, I stopped on the cliff road right beneath this house, thrust both hands in the air and yelled, "Praise the Lord." How wonderful God is to us. We do not move until March.

As I prayed at the bedside, a great circle of red glow surrounded me. The Lord still forbids opening a window at night and keeps indicating that the evil one is after us, but he is carefully and completely protecting us. Last night the colors and glory of the Holy Spirit circulated all over the room—all night. Every time I awakened either colored light or the fog or the smoke of the Holy Spirit were visible.

December 25, 1988 –

We are on the way to Florida today after a peaceful Christmas filled with celebrations of Jesus' birth in church services and programs. The Candlelight Communion Service last evening was especially moving.

Amazingly enough, there were several green leaves left on the sweet gum tree when we started south. We have had two snows and many cold, below-freezing nights.

At the last moment I bought and examined the final yearly pictograph of *Life* magazine for 1988. Again the Lord sent the message, *"No one who puts a hand to the plow and looks back is fit for the kingdom of God"* (Lk 9:62). I threw it away.

January 4, 1989 –

I partially awakened in the night and looked up into the brightest light I have ever seen. It was so blinding I closed my eyes for protection. I knew immediately it was God because he dwells in unapproachable light.

This morning the hymnal opened in my hand to the great old hymn about God the Father, "Immortal, Invisible," by Walter Chalmers Smith. "Immortal, invisible, God only wise, *in light inaccessible hid from our eyes,* most blessed, most glorious, the ancient of days, almighty, victorious, thy great name we praise."

January 8, 1989—

This morning we heard that a bad snowstorm was assaulting the Dakotas. The Lord had sent a song during the night, "Snow is falling; snow on snow ... " The Lord is so close to us. He lives with us and tells us what is going on and what we should do.

At church I saw the smoke of the Holy Spirit surround the minister as he spoke of Jesus. He said we must read Ezekiel 33:8-9 every day for it will make a difference in what we say to our friends. *If I say to the wicked, "O wicked ones, you shall surely die," and you do not speak to warn the wicked to turn from their ways, the wicked shall die in their iniquity, but their blood I will require at your hand. But if you warn the wicked to turn from their ways, and they do not turn from their ways, the wicked shall die in their iniquity, but you will have saved your life.*

January 11, 1989—

Many times while worshipping God, lights flash and flames and clouds appear in my spirit vision. Smith Wigglesworth, the great early 20th century English evangelist, said one cannot get that healing from heaven without going to heaven after it. Healing only comes to the call of a person deep in prayer, praise and worship. First you have to get God's attention.

January 14, 1989 –

While listening to Alexander Scourby read from the Old Testament, I was startled by a passage in Zephaniah 3:9: *At that time I will change the speech of the peoples to a pure speech, that all of them may call on the name of the Lord and serve him with one accord.* I stopped in my tracks. This seems to be a prophecy of the "tongues" that occurs in the New Testament after the wrath of God has been assuaged and people all over the world turn to him in trust, love, humility and faithfulness.

It is possible that all earthly languages are impure, abused, no longer clean enough to use in praising the Lord. So he had to send a new language that has never been fouled. Even the person with the gift of interpretation does not know the literal translation of the "other tongue." Since this language is sent by the Holy Spirit, it is pure and undefiled.

I know the Spirit sends it because he makes my lips twitch in a way I have never before experienced. This has happened often recently. I felt it strongly when the earthquake occurred in the Soviet Union. The only way to relieve the twitch is to pray in "tongues," then the twitch ceases.

Another theological truth came to me from something I found in 2 Timothy: *Proclaim the message; be persistent whether the time is favorable or unfavorable; convince, rebuke, and encourage, with the utmost patience in teaching* (4:2). If we do this, God will take care of the healing we need. We do his work and he takes care of us. Praise God!

January 20, 1989 –

The Lord keeps sending hymns like "My Shepherd Will Supply My Need" and "Trust and Obey" to say he is taking care of my knees which are sore and swollen. He is also telling me to write to my unsaved friends and tell them about him for the time is short. Another message that came this morning is a comfort. God said, "Fenced cities—I am to you, a fence."

January 26, 1989—

This morning we were hiking at Corkscrew National Audubon Park near Ft. Myers on the boardwalk a long way from a rest room—which I needed badly. I remembered Nancy telling about a time in Canada when she needed a rest room but one was not available, so she asked the Lord to condense it, and he did. So I asked the Lord to help me in that way.

Thankfully he did and I felt no other urgency until we finished the tour at our leisure. Then I thought, the Lord can do this easily and wants to help us. So I asked him to send circulation to my knees to relieve the pain and soreness. Another recent message from the Lord was, *"My grace is sufficient for your needs"* (paraphrased from 2 Cor 12:9) or was it "knees?"

February 4, 1989—

This morning the Lord said, *"Within the veil!"* What a magnificent message! He has been preparing me for this. This is the reason I must give up worldly influences and activities for inside the holy of holies I must be able to receive messages from the Lord to give the people. What an awesome responsibility!

February 12, 1989—

I awakened in the night to a medium tenor voice calling my name once. I said, "Here I am; is there a message?" But there was no message or perhaps the voice was the message.

My knees are coming around. I walked at least a mile today. The Lord is healing the irritation and inflammation and the exercises I am doing are strengthening them. Praise God!

February 16, 1989—

I attended the Wednesday night prayer service at a nearby church. The minister told of a member of the church, a 17-year-old boy who had been in a bad automobile accident and received a crushed skull. He was pronounced hopeless by the doctors, but his family and the members of the church gathered and prayed fervently for him. Two weeks later he came to church, stood before the congregation and testified to his healing by the Lord. Praise God!

Today I discovered a prophecy of the end times from Joel: *Then afterward I will pour out my spirit on all flesh; your sons and your daughters shall prophesy, your old men shall dream dreams, and your young men shall see visions. ... I will show portents in the heavens and on the earth, **blood and fire and columns of smoke** ... before the great and terrible day of the Lord comes* (2:28-31). Since I am seeing blood and fire and vapor of smoke at night, could the end be soon?

February 20, 1989—

We are back in the Tallahassee for a few days and had a glorious experience at the Wakulla Methodist Church last night. The minister and church officers called us forward to the altar, laid hands on us and prayed, then they held a reception in our honor after church. We felt thoroughly comforted and loved.

We were so filled with the Holy Spirit that after we retired, the Lord sent waves and blankets of color. He also sent warm sensations over my whole body. The Lord is so good.

February 28, 1989—

Much has happened. When we returned home after two tiring days of driving from Baton Rouge, I had a severe attack of high blood pressure. Howard took me to the hospital emergency room twice but they didn't keep me. Sunday night I thought I would die. My ears were ringing, my chest hurt, I couldn't breathe and both arms were numb. My friend Hazel, who has the gift of prophecy, called Miriam and told her I was near death—and so did the Lord tell me. Both friends prayed for me all night and I am sure Howard prayed also.

In the midst of this, blankets of light came in the window and rolled over me, sending a tingling warmth through my body. The light came in colors, one after another: violet, carnelian red, emerald green, blue, creamy white and amber. I was almost certain I was dying because these are the rainbow colors around the throne of God that John wrote of in Revelation.

I said to God, "If it is your will that I come to you, I'll be glad to see you; however I'd like to stay and live in my new house, write books and do other things including take care of Howard. It's up to you." At that point, trusting God for either life or death, I began to relax.

The lights continued to roll in, sometimes bright and sometimes barely visible. The bed and my whole insides shook with the quivering rhythm of the Holy Spirit. About midnight, a bright light came into the room. It had no definable form—just a blob of fog or vapor. I felt as if my whole body were lifted off the bed!

Naturally, I thought, "This is it! I am on my way to the next world!" Instead a powerful wave of heat went through my body and I felt as if I were being toasted from the inside out. Though it was quite hot, it was not painful. The heat settled in my abdomen and chest. I don't know how long it lasted, but when it passed I found myself on the bed—still alive. All light had disappeared, but left in the room was a thick heavy fog or smoke which remained all night.

Two days later I was admitted to the hospital where my medication was adjusted and a number of tests were run on my heart and kidneys. Both functions are normal. I am convinced that the God of the Universe saved my life and kept me from having heart and kidney damage because of the prayers of my husband and friends. Praise God!

March 6, 1989—

While in the hospital I worshipped the Lord almost continuously. I sang, praised, prayed and thought about the Lord the entire time. My friend Hazel came to see me and delivered a message from the Lord which said (paraphrased): "Keep in hourly contact with me. You are to rest 15 days and are not to make plans for the future. Just live one day at a time with Howard. I have cleansed you from evil."

She also said the Lord instructed me to take Communion so I called the church and one of the ministers brought Communion to me. I felt the Holy Spirit enter my body during that service. God keeps reminding me, *"Though thousands stumble and fall beside you and tens of thousands around you perish, still it will not come nigh you"* (paraphrased from Ps 91:7).

One night recently I felt an asthma attack coming on. I knew struggling to breathe would increase my blood pressure and the asthma medicine would also make it go up, so in desperation, I said to God, "You can heal me, if you will."

He answered and said distinctly, "I can and I will." Just then a vapor formed in front of my face and came toward me, disappearing in my nostrils as I inhaled. My lungs cleared up instantly and I breathed deeply and safely all night. Praise God! [The asthma has never returned.]

March 13, 1989—

Two nights in a row I have awakened in the Spirit with a strange sensation. Everything around me looked grainy and pebbly and I felt as though I were being held tightly by something and I didn't want to move. The Lord told me today that healing comes faster when we are in the Spirit.

March 15, 1989—

The Lord sent a song, an old tune with new words. To the tune of "Revive Us Again" he sent these words: "To Jesus we go, to Jesus we reach, to Jesus we answer and Jesus we touch. Hallelujah, thine the glory; hallelujah, amen. Hallelujah, thine the glory, revive us again."

March 21, 1989—

I am sitting by the window in our new house. We are being moved today. It is so peaceful and beautiful. Howard, bless him, is doing all the work and I am merely observing.

Yesterday we received some pictures of our lovely little goddaughter. In return, I sent her parents a prayer for them to say in her presence every morning: "Child's Morning Hymn," by Rebecca Weston. "Father, we thank thee for the night, and for the pleasant morning light; for rest and food and loving care, and all that makes the world so fair. Help us to do the things we should, to be to others kind and good, in all we do, in work or play, to love thee better day by day. Amen."

I prayed for Gary last night asking Jesus to go to him as he did to Paul in such a vivid way that Gary will be convinced— for he has not given up the defiant spirit he has had all his life. This morning God showed me by sending a hymn, "I'll Go Where You Want Me To Go," that my assignment is to speak to Gary about Jesus. God help me for he doesn't want to listen.

April 1, 1989–

Yesterday Miriam wanted to see me so I made a time and went by. I told her that I felt like Jonah who had fled from the Lord's assignment. Rather than witness to Gary, I had gotten into trouble going to Florida and getting very sick. But Miriam had received a message from the Lord and she trembled, cried and her hands burned while telling what the Lord said. "I am taking Gary to heaven because of your prayers. You do not have to go back to the city, but you may go if you wish. You are so special to me that even the angels are longing for the completed kingdom."

Two days ago I had a vision of many levels, as in venetian blinds, when the name Gary came to mind. After that the hymn, "Victory in Jesus," rolled into my consciousness and I thought Gary might be dying.

April 2, 1989–

Gary died last night. I saw heavenly lights all night and felt a tremendous wave of heat travel through my body this morning. Gary must have given his life to Jesus at the last minute and is now meeting the Lord. I hope this is pleasant and that Gary is allowed to use his creative mind in helping the Lord.

April 8, 1989–

I just found two important passages in Isaiah: *Is not this the fast that I choose: to loose the bonds of injustice, to undo the thongs of the yoke, to let the oppressed go free, and to break every yoke? Is it not to share your bread with the hungry, and bring the homeless poor into your house; when you see the naked, to cover them, and not to hide yourself from your own kin? Then your light shall break forth like the dawn, and **your healing shall***

spring up quickly; *your vindicator shall go before you, the glory of the Lord shall be your rear guard. Then you shall call, and the Lord will answer; you shall cry for help, and he will say, Here I am* (58:6-9).

This reminds me of what Jesus said about helping others in Matthew 25. The other passage in Isaiah that impressed me was: *If you refrain from trampling the Sabbath, from pursuing your own interests on my holy day; if you call the Sabbath a delight and the holy day of the Lord honorable; if you honor it, not going your own ways, serving your own interests, or pursuing your own affairs; then you shall take delight in the Lord, and I will make you ride upon the heights of the earth; I will feed you with the heritage of your ancestor Jacob, for the mouth of the Lord has spoken* (58:13-14). [Much later I started practicing the precepts of this passage, attempting to do and say only what Jesus might do or say on Sunday, the day of rest and worship.]

June 5, 1989–

Some interesting precepts are found in Job: *"Then, if there should be for one of them an angel, a mediator, one of a thousand, one who declares a person upright, and he is gracious to that person, and says, 'Deliver him from going down into the Pit; I have found a ransom; let his flesh become fresh with youth; let him return to the days of his youthful vigor.' Then he prays to God, and is accepted by him, he comes into his presence with joy, and God repays him for his righteousness. That person sings to others and says, 'I sinned, and perverted what was right, and it was not paid back to me. He has redeemed my soul from going down to the Pit, and my life shall see the light.' God indeed does all these things, twice, three times, with mortals, to bring back their souls from the Pit, so that they may see the light of life"* (33:23-30).

There are several revelations in this passage: first, the mention of a ransom—Jesus, the Christ; then the saved one shall have flesh like a child, a youth. [It was while in the spirit that I saw my own face change to a youthful face. This, no doubt, is the way we will look in heaven.] Third, the point being made in the last section is that each person is given at least three opportunities to be saved from final destruction.

June 30, 1989—

I have started praying fervently for our city and all its suburbs. Since the Lord told Joshua he could have every place he set his foot (Josh 1:3), I have claimed this promise and have driven around our town, claiming it for Jesus and declaring that no evil can remain in the name of Jesus, praying and praising God in Psalms and songs. I ordered evil out in the name of Jesus and invited God in. The feeling of his acceptance of my efforts flooded my heart. Then this afternoon, awaking from a nap, I heard the Lord say, "God is on this mountain!"

July 15, 1989—

Last night I saw three bright lights in a row shoot toward me. One was red, one gold and the other white. I am always in the Spirit when seeing such things. No doubt this stood for the Trinity of God—Father, Son and Holy Spirit.

August 1, 1989—

In talking with Jenny and Max today, I agreed to tutor their son Tom once a week. Thinking about this brought chills to me because I had been dreaming for many nights about a baby given into my keeping, but didn't know the meaning of the dream until I agreed to tutor Tom. He is the baby. I trust the Lord will help us use this time together effectively. I felt as though the Lord were saying "amen" to it. [Later, I turned this job over to Howard and the two have a friendship going now.]

August 30, 1989—

While listening to the book of Isaiah on tape, my head started feeling electrified during the great passage where Hezekiah was told he would be given 15 more years of life. I know the Lord is offering me extra time at the end to do things I want to do and things he wants me to do.

September 8, 1989—

By an unusual circumstance, I saw an old woman bent double, looking at the ground as she walked. I hurried up to her. The younger woman at her side turned out to be her daughter. I asked the younger woman if I might pray for her mother. She was very suspicious and tried to discourage me, but I persisted. Finally she allowed me to touch the old woman. I said a short two-sentence prayer of healing for her back and mind. (The daughter told me she had Alzheimer's disease.) Then the daughter started the car and they drove off. I barely retrieved my Bible and purse from the hood of the car, but the Lord had sent me and I was obedient. Praise God!

September 9, 1989—

When I opened the window for fresh air last night, I saw columns of fog in the yard—at least two. I then knew we were being protected from the evil one so I closed the window and went peacefully to sleep.

During the night, I asked the Lord to touch my hand and stretched out my right hand across the bed. The left one I laid on my heart. *Switch!* The Lord touched the left hand! Heat and prickles like electricity flooded the hand on my heart—the

Lord has such a wonderful sense of humor. How is it that the Lord of the Universe is so close to me? I barely breathe a request when it is granted! This reminds me of the Scriptural passage from Isaiah *You [God] meet those who gladly do right, those who remember you in your ways* (64:5).

September 14, 1989 –

The Lord awakened me this morning at five with the hymn "Sweet Hour of Prayer," so I put on a robe, gathered a blanket around me and went to the family room. I prayed and listened for an hour, then went back to bed. Before that, in the night, I was awakened with the presence of an angel beside the bed. A brief fraction of a second before fading into fog and disappearing, a woman with blond hair appeared to me.

I made some kind of noise and Howard awakened and asked if I was all right. When I answered, the figure was gone, but what was left was a glorious light in the window and wave after wave of warmth. At one point a bright light shot toward me until I closed my eyes against the glare. Immediately, I felt my whole body seized by something and thought I would be taken away, but the feeling faded. This gift must have been given because I spoke to a very old friend about his salvation.

September 15, 1989 –

I experienced the most wonderful fellowship with God last night. Waking about four with light sweeping over the bed, I felt my whole body become tingly and warm. Many waves of this flooded over me for about an hour. At five this faded. I asked the Lord if I should get up and pray, but he said, "No, we have already had fellowship and you should sleep." I did, bless him.

Later I began reading something the Lord led me to which

mentioned that one should immediately obey rather than argue or postpone the instruction. That is one of my failings.

September 16, 1989—

After working in the yard all morning, I drove to the church this afternoon, prayed for half an hour, anointed the sanctuary, went to the hospital to see two sick friends, then to the home of another who was sick. I anointed all of them with oil by handing them the bottle of prayed-over oil and asking them to anoint themselves.

This method seems less threatening or condescending, as it puts everyone on an equal basis. [One of these was dying of bone cancer. She has slowly recovered and now seems to be in remission. The other two were less seriously ill, and they have recovered also.]

October 7, 1989—

Whenever the Lord sends a signal, I drive around the city and pray. I did today. It is about 30 miles around all the suburbs of this small city. I prayed, praised and claimed all of Bartlesville for Jesus. It felt so good and I'm certain it was accepted by God. As the drive was ending, I asked the Lord to send a cloud by day and fire by night over the city for its protection.

October 8, 1989—

At three this morning I received word to rise and pray. Gathering a blanket I went into the family room, prayed and sang praises to God—quietly. After an hour I looked out the window. In the Spirit I saw the flickering flames of the Holy Spirit over the valley, just as I had asked. God is so good.

October 31, 1989 —

So many tragedies have occurred during the past two weeks: a terrible earthquake struck San Francisco; a hurricane devastated Charleston, South Carolina; an explosion and fire killed many people in Houston; my friend Nancy has a son with cancer in his lungs; a young woman who grew up in the church has burns on most of her body; another woman in town was severely injured in an automobile crash; and the Navy has had four serious accidents in three days.

Prayers for the city came none too soon and certainly must be continued regularly. The entire nation needs prayer. I continue to rise and pray early every morning. One morning, as I was waking to beautiful lights and a pebbly vision, I heard a series of notes on a rising scale on a harp! Praise God.

November 10, 1989 —

Today after planting daffodil bulbs, I went to Heritage Manor to lead gospel hymn singing. An old Chinese woman, new among the residents, cannot speak English, so I can imagine how lonely she gets. Since my neighbor has lived in China and speaks Chinese, perhaps she will go with me to talk to Chu Chen. [My neighbor did go with me to visit her and it turned out she spoke the Mandarin Chinese dialect so could converse. We could tell Chu was delighted to hear a sound of home.]

November 24, 1989 —

One day I asked the Lord about my Jewish friend, Sandra. Later he said, "Rahab"—who was a resident of Jericho and was spared, along with her household, when Joshua invaded that city (Josh 6:17-25). She later lived among the Israelites and was an ancestor of Jesus (Mt 1:5). Because of this message, I believe my friend will be saved at the last minute.

November 30, 1989—

We are in the camper again, heading for Florida for a brief visit with our church friends at Wakulla. I had thought the Lord said it was all right to go.

I awakened last night to several waves of Spirit going through me. Just as I was becoming alert, I saw a blank check! The Lord was asking what I wanted. Immediately, without thinking, I asked for good health. I will ponder this gift and tuck it down in my secret place to meditate on occasionally before spending. What a fantastic vision!

December 1, 1989—

I have come to the conclusion that the Lord has made me for himself. He has slowly stripped away everything I have always thought to be important so I might be totally his and dedicate myself completely to him. Gently and lovingly he has taken away Christmas trees, football, movies, plays, reading anything but Bible or good religious commentary, television, even bird-watching to a certain extent. At the same time he took away these things I loved, he also took away complaining, anger and fear. In return he has given me his word, his presence, the most profound joy and a deeper appreciation of natural beauty: the sky, clouds, beautiful trees and leaves, flowers, birds, animals, grasses, sand, sea and mountain. He has filled my bosom with singing, worship, prayer, love, compassion, teaching, laughter, insight and empathy, acute sensitivity, sounds, visions and smells of heaven. He has revealed to me his face and the knowledge of his love and forgiveness, the gifts of healing and miracles, the spiritual fruits of love and forgiveness, fearlessness and assurance that he is completely in control of everything in this universe down to my life. Amen.

December 5, 1989 –

A dear friend has become involved in Silva Mind Control, and I am concerned that she might lose her salvation. The Lord said to write her a letter.

Dear Francine,

Thanks for your letter and the information about Silva Mind Control. We are in Wildwood, Florida, for a couple of weeks visiting friends and relatives. Howard is napping and I am thinking while the warm sun comes in the window.

Francine, I know you are a dedicated Christian, but I believe this Silva training has taken you off on a philosophy that is moving in another direction. Please know that I care a great deal about you and wish not to hurt you or to hurt our friendship. However, the Lord has been asking me to write this letter for at least two years and I must be obedient.

Hebrew-Christian doctrine speaks of the Kingdom of God. God told Samuel in the Old Testament that the people were not rejecting him, Samuel, when they asked for a king, but were rejecting God as their ruler. Jesus came declaring the Kingdom of God to be at hand. It has – with his life, death, and resurrection – become possible for ordinary people to be in touch with God in order for him to rule over them and instruct them and judge them. We are do God's will in our lives, not our own will.

As I understand Silva, devotees are supposed to decide what they want and how they want to live, then with mental manipulation (states of consciousness) control their own bodies and to some extent their own circumstances. This leaves God and his will for our lives out of the picture.

Forgive a personal question, but it is necessary to make a point. Do you still read and study the Bible, pray to God and listen to his instructions for your life decisions before you decide what to do? Or do you decide what you want, then proceed to try to make it happen with your mind through altered states of consciousness?

There are many spirits active in this world. Not all of them are of God. Some that are not on God's side pretend to be in order to trap people and channel them out of his realm. When we meditate without first praising God and asking his will, we are opening up to any spirit that happens to be around and we stand in danger of picking up spirits contrary to God.

The purpose of life is to know God and praise him continuously, as 1 Thessalonians says: *Rejoice always, pray without ceasing, give thanks in all circumstances; for this is the will of God in Christ Jesus for you. Do not quench the Spirit. Do not despise the words of prophets, but test everything; hold fast to what is good; abstain from every form of evil* (5:16-22).

Living under God's kingship brings the most incredible joy and peace in one's life. It also brings a supreme confidence; one is never afraid again. No artificial programming can bring this kind of joy and peace. I hope you rethink this issue and decide to put self-programming aside and turn to God alone for your life decisions.

Love,
Dottie G.

[Francine has never contacted me again.]

December 10, 1989—

Silently we stood near the entrance of St. Mark's National Wildlife Refuge at that magical moment just before dusk. Birds were shifting from one side of the road to another, limpkins screamed in the distant swamp, a barred owl called, ducks and gulls were making a last pass before settling into a quiet pond to roost and the late afternoon sun shone on some beautiful yellow flowers against a background of red leaves—a reminder of summer in the arms of autumn. The Lord is so good to us.

December 13, 1989—

We had to cut short our two-week vacation in Florida because chronic high blood pressure tightened its grip on my body two days ago. A visit to the Tallahassee hospital emergency room left me with more pills and warnings, so we decided to come home in as short a time as possible.

As Howard drove through rain, I lay on the gaucho couch and thought about the mystical moments we had experienced at St. Mark's Refuge and wondered if I would live to experience any more such times in God's natural world. We have spent many vacations in the wild areas of America and loved every minute. I asked, "Lord, am I going to die right away?"

"No, my daughter," came the reply deep inside me.

"I know," I said, "that you moved the sundial back ten degrees to assure King Hezekiah he would live. But I don't have a sundial, and if I did, it wouldn't work in this rainstorm in the middle of Interstate 10."

While Howard stopped to get gas, I glanced at the clock on the camper wall. It read 10:25 A.M. A little later back on the highway, Howard turned to ask the time. I looked again, read the clock and said, "10:25." Immediately, I knew something strange and unusual was happening.

"No," he said, "it's later than that." He reached on a shelf for his watch and read it. "It's 10:35," he said. "Your watch is *ten minutes* slow."

I quickly checked the camper clock and my wrist watch. Both read 10:25 A.M. I laughed and laughed—and am still laughing. God didn't manufacture a sundial, hand it to me and clear out a hundred miles of rain. He merely turned back my watch and the camper clock ten minutes. How wonderful the Lord is!

One night that I was so sick, I lay in the camper listening to Matthew's gospel. I was really into it, hearing and feeling every word. It was raining outside and I felt prickles on my skin— like cold drops of water. I stood up and felt the ceiling around the bolts above my head to see if it were leaking. No! Then I knew the prickles were from the spiritual dimension—an angel or the Lord. Amazing!

December 15, 1989—

The Lord is sending angels to protect us at night. I saw one outside the bedroom window last night. A light was behind his head. I saw no features, just a mass of fog shaped like a man.

I talked to my old friend Hazel, who has the gift of prophecy. She said the Lord would heal me and that I should rest and stay home. The Lord's message to her was that I would live for a while, then go to heaven, then return with Christ to earth. The Lord says he has things for me to do here in this life. The tone of the message was the Lord's assurance that I was completely his and would not turn back. It was like conversation with an intimate friend—not the usual commanding tone.

December 18, 1989—

Jesus said to my spirit that God's love will heal me. If I accept it totally, I'll be healed totally; if only partially, then I will be partially healed. He also said for me to stay away from social contacts for a month.

I opened the Bible and the Lord directed me to Psalm 62: *For God alone my soul waits in silence, for my hope is from him. He alone is my rock and my salvation, my fortress; I shall not be shaken. On God rests my deliverance and my honor; my mighty rock, my refuge is in God* (5-7).

December 20, 1989—

The Lord was present in light, color and electricity all night. I actually felt electricity travel through my head twice and awakened with waves of Spirit rolling over my body like surf at the seacoast. The bed also shook to the rhythm of the flames of the Holy Spirit. At one point a bright light came into the room and disappeared into my eye. With power the Holy Spirit is coming to me!

December 24, 1989—

How difficult it is to be perfectly righteous! While listening to sacred music this morning, I noticed the Lord was absent. I started thinking about what I had done and asked Jesus to make me aware of it.

Soon he brought four things to my attention: 1. I spoke an unkind word about my aunt to my sister, Betty. What I said was true but unnecessary. 2. I did the same to Jenny about a person in the church. Also true, also unwarranted. 3. I turned on television news when the Lord asked me not to watch television today, Sunday. 4. I ate too much rich food tonight after he asked me to eat lightly. [I was to learn the next day that an important message was coming, and the Lord wanted me to be able to hear it above the workings of my insides.]

December 25, 1989—

Early this morning the Lord said to my inner being, *"Don't celebrate Christmas!"* I must really be sick to hear something like that. As I pondered the message, he started rolling through my mind a remembrance of the Christmas cards Howard and I had made the first several years of our marriage—there was a madonna we had made using a wood cut, a photograph of a church in the mountains, a candle being reflected by mirrors into infinity, a desert scene in silk screen, then a waterfall in silkscreen with the message, "Let justice roll down like a river and righteousness like an everflowing stream." At this point the visions stopped and remained on the waterfall. That, he said, is *his message of Christmas!*

I hate, I despise your festivals, and I take no delight in your solemn assemblies. Even though you offer me your burnt offerings and grain offerings, I will not accept them; and the offerings of well-being of your fatted animals I will not look upon. Take away from me the noise of your songs; I will not listen to the melody of your harps. But let justice roll down like waters, and righteousness like an everflowing stream (Am 5:21-25).

Looking with his eyes and with the background of his word to Amos, I am beginning to understand what God is saying. He cannot stand the hoopla, the drunken celebrations, the lies, the abuse, the overspending of the rich on meaningless presents, the condescension to the poor, the overeating, the phoney piety— all in his name. He would much rather have people turn to him in true repentance and start living in righteousness and true justice. And especially love.

I listened again to the "Bells" tape which started this series of notebooks and hidden in the middle of it, almost overlooked in the excitement of chiming bells from heaven, was a clear statement by Hazel, quoting the Lord to me, saying, *"I am in the midst of making you a prophet!"*

What a message to America—*Don't Celebrate Christmas!*

[That I should be given a message from God for America was beyond my wildest imagination, yet more than a year later I was given the second of three messages from the Lord not only to America but also to the world.]

December 27, 1989—

I went to bed early last night. Perhaps a half-hour later my body started getting hot, particularly my chest. It was Spirit heat which I felt before when several people prayed for me simultaneously during my facial cancer episode. I had to roll down the covers for about an hour until the heat slowly drifted away and I went to sleep. I knew someone had been praying fervently for me. Perhaps it was Howard who has been so sweet and solicitous of my wants and needs.

January 3, 1990 –

The Lord has been preparing me for the message that came today. He said by way of a hymn, "O Zion Haste," that I am to write a book. He kept rolling the phrase, "Publish glad tidings, tidings of peace; tidings of Jesus' redemption and release." At the same time, the Holy Spirit has been guiding my mind to the realization that I am to glean my notebooks and write a synopsis of my experiences with the Lord. He has sent a hymn to assure of his presence during the writing: "Through It All," by Andrea Crouch. "Through it all, I've learned to trust in Jesus; I've learned to trust in God. ... I've learned to depend upon God's Word."

January 11, 1990 –

Last night I awakened in the Spirit. Everything looked pebbly and I saw faces at the ceiling—many faces. Light was moving around in the room so I knew the faces were angels. I laughed and watched joyfully. As I continued to waken, the Spirit state diminished and the vision disappeared.

February 4, 1990 –

I have been attending a prayer and healing service Thursday evenings. One Thursday morning the Lord told me I should take a little six-year old boy, the son of a friend, to the service with me and request prayer for his ears. It was raining that night but we went anyway. Miriam accompanied me and we took the lad forward for prayer. On the way home I talked to him in normal tones and *he could hear.* Praise God! The Lord approved mightily and sent lights and colors all night.

February 14, 1990—

Last night I started seeing visions showing jagged edges, sharp teeth, red points and chaos. I ordered Satan out in the name of Jesus and the visions disappeared, but the strangest thing happened—a grass and brush fire started in the wilderness area beyond our housing development and raged out of control for several hours, coming quite close to some of the houses. I prayed, reminding the Lord that he had brought us up here, and he wasn't going to let our house burn. I ordered the fire out and gone from this mountain in the name of Jesus. In the meantime, four fire department units arrived and brought the fire under control. Nobody lost a home. After prayer today, I anointed the entire house.

February 15, 1990—

The Lord came to me last night in beautiful light showing three foggy faces on the ceiling, revealing they are the angels who are protecting this house and telling us not to worry.

February 27, 1990—

Today is my sister's 66th birthday. I sent a card yesterday noon and it was in her hand by today noon. Either the Holy Spirit or angels helped it arrive on time because it could not make it that fast by ordinary mail. At least it never has before.

March 6, 1990—

I spent part of the day yesterday counseling a friend. The Lord was so pleased, he sent waves of colored lights all over the room as soon as I went to bed. I looked at the ceiling and saw wheels whirling again. At first they turned counter-clockwise, then later clockwise. There is never a rim, only very fine spokes. In the night I partially awakened to see a huge person beside the bed. I went back to sleep remembering having seen someone—a man—in the room. Strangely, I was not afraid.

Later, during wakeful periods, I prayed for the friend I had counseled and her husband because evil seemed abroad in the night. Miriam told me this morning that her Bible study class teacher had mentioned feeling much evil in the town last night.

March 23, 1990—

Surprise! A wild turkey walked through the yard yesterday. It wandered around both front and back for a half-hour before disappearing into the vacant lot beside us. Howard snapped a picture of it through the window. It is so pleasant up here overlooking the whole world—safe, dry, warm and cozy.

We have spent much time and energy setting up a vegetable garden on a level spot near the cliff. The pansies are now blooming as well as the azalea bushes we just planted.

Miriam called to say God told her that something I am involved in has *three parts*. [Though it meant nothing to either of us at the time, I learned later that the Lord was referring to the prophecy he gave at Christmas and was advising there were three prophecies—two more to come.]

A tick bit me a few days ago. I found it in my right groin, encircled by a red spot the size of a dime. As I started pulling it off with tweezers, it fell off and disintegrated. Amazing! The spot never did itch or hurt.

March 29, 1990—

I attended a prayer service tonight at the home of a friend. The leader had been reading the book of Acts and made the observation that all who had a Damascus road experience were due for much suffering and had a mission to perform.

I will never forget a similar experience in May 1973. I was

on private property—a wooded hillside ten miles from town—engaged in making a breeding bird survey of 40 acres of undisturbed woodland. Compass in hand I trekked back and forth across the plot, stopping frequently to listen for bird calls. The only sound besides the birds which interrupted the silence was the wind and an occasional squirrel. Listening intently I could imagine sounds made by Indians during the centuries before.

Approaching a small canyon where water dropped 25 feet to sandstone before trickling down the hillside, I stepped up on a flat rock to watch the water. Suddenly a golden glow descended on me with a shimmering light. At the same time my knees became weak and I had to sit down to keep from falling.

No one spoke to me but all around was a vibrating glistening light. I sat in the midst of that light for many minutes feeling ecstatic—a deep sense of joy and peace and especially love for God. The state of ecstasy continued for about two weeks.

I could not know until many years later that this baptism singled me out for a special mission for God. Part of the mission is the writing of this book.

April 25, 1990—

"Like a bridge over troubled waters, I will lay me down," was the phrase in song that came today. Jesus wants to be my bridge over troubled waters. Thank you, Lord.

Last night I saw the Crystal Sea again. It looked like cut glass of the most intricate variety. This time the sea was in color—green. The Lord has sent wonderful waves of Spirit and visions. This morning I awakened to see a column of fire at the window. At the same time I felt the Holy Spirit surge of electricity. God is so good!

May 13, 1990—

Our mountain was alive with bird songs yesterday and today. For worship tonight, Pastor Allen chose Psalm 98 which says, "The hills shall sing with joy together before the Lord." It reminded me of our own singing hill this weekend.

The Lord sent me a dream of a brown creeper climbing up the bathroom wall to say that migrant warblers were right here on our mountain so I wouldn't have to drive 40 miles to see them. Rising early I drove to the backside of the mountain, parked and started walking down the gravel road.

Soon the delicate high trills and melodies of singing warblers rose from the steep hillside to greet me. There was a parula warbler zipping up the scale and a yellow warbler singing, "Sweet, sweet, I'm so sweet." On the other side of the road a Canada warbler uttered his typical attention-getting "check," before singing a tuneless jumble of notes. A Baltimore oriole's high, sweet flute-like notes hung from the top of a sycamore across the way where he has established his place and his bright orange breast attracted the morning sun.

By mid-morning, the singing of birds had diminished and I wandered back to the car. At the edge of a clearing a bluebird flew in front of me, stopped on a limb above the road and sang, "Cheer, dearie—cheer, dearie."

"Yes," I said.

May 22, 1990—

I have started a project of memorizing Psalms. Saying them in quiet moments provides a place for the mind to go instead of the stream of consciousness garbage that seeps in.

May 26, 1990—

There is a ring of brown grass on the front lawn. I thought

at first it was poisoned by a satanic group which has done mischief on this mountain before—including throwing dead animals against our front door. But I found out the Lord sent the ring to assure us of his protection.

Soon after waking I saw a golden circle on the ceiling, about the size of a headband or crown. [Since then I have seen a golden circle on the ceiling each morning when I waken.] Periodically I walk around our entire yard singing Psalms, declaring that our land belongs to Jesus so no evil can touch us.

Psalm 91:9-14 assures us, *Because you have made the Lord your refuge, the Most High your dwelling place, no evil shall befall you, no scourge come near your tent. For he will command his angels concerning you to guard you in all your ways. On their hands they will bear you up, so that you will not dash your foot against a stone. You will tread on the lion and the adder, the young lion and the serpent you will trample under foot.*

June 10, 1990—

One night recently I awakened to see the whole sky aflame out the double window above the trees. This must be in answer to the prayer request for God to send a cloud by day and fire by night over the city. It is amazing what God will do if we ask in simple faith and trust.

The joy of his nearness is a powerful balm to all troubles and illnesses.

The Lord was powerfully present with me when I went to traffic court to answer for backing into someone and damaging her fender. I explained how it happened and the judge suspended the fine. Praise God! This could only occur because friends were praying for me the entire time.

June 24, 1990—

I have been thinking about creation versus evolution for a long time, recently in detail. I asked the Lord and he sent a hymn containing the expression, "God has created all things."

So I said, "OK, Lord, I know you created everything, but did you do it in seven literal days or seven aeons?"

The answer came this morning. As I walked to the garden the Lord sent the hymn "O God, Our Help in Ages Past." I started humming the tune, then the words to the fourth stanza came to me. *"A thousand ages in thy sight are like an evening gone."* There is the answer! The seven days are God's days and may be as long as he wants them. So the world and its inhabitants were created in six of God's days—with humans on the sixth day. Things did not evolve by themselves but God made changes as he saw fit. But humans were given special souls with which to communicate with God.

June 30, 1990—

A vision of beautiful green stones appeared above my head last night. The color grew more intense until the center became a pattern of shining green emeralds of sublime beauty. Today I picked up the *National Geographic* and saw an article about emeralds—the pictures looked exactly like my vision. The Lord anticipated my activities and was showing that he creates all things, including emeralds. Bless him!

July 31, 1990—

Some time ago the Lord sent some visions with the message that the Antichrist is here on earth now. Since I couldn't figure out who it was, I laid that knowledge aside. Last weekend I saw a short TV segment on Rev. Sun Myung Moon's Unification Church movement. Monday when the church women were kneeling in prayer, someone mentioned Rev. Moon. Immediately the Lord nudged me. Could he be either *the* Antichrist or *an* Antichrist? If so, *the world will end soon.* According to 1 John 4:3: *And every spirit that does not confess Jesus is not from God. And this is the spirit of the Antichrist, of which you have heard that is coming; and now it is already in the world.*

All the hurricanes, wild fires, tornadoes, earthquakes, droughts, famines, floods, epidemics and other disasters point to the end time. I am guessing *it may come early next century.*

August 20, 1990–

It came to me tonight that the world really is going to end soon! The Middle East is about to explode. People are fleeing and will continue to flee—as I saw in visions. The Antichrist has already been named. The Holy Spirit has anointed many with fire and power and tongues. I just reread a previous notebook and saw an entry where the Lord said the end is near. (As I write this, green light spreads across the page and my hand.)

August 27, 1990–

Last week I passed out handbills for the Jay Strack revival crusade. Our church has been given a territory to cover—house to house—so it took four separate trips to complete my assignment. The first day I reached for a stack of handbills to take around the block when something said, "That's not enough." So I took more. As it turned out, it was the exact number needed to cover the block, both sides of the street, all duplexes. There must have been 50 residences. Also, the Lord sent a cool breeze when I became very hot since it was over 100° F.

September 1, 1990–

When Iraq took over Kuwait and the United Nations started

sending troops to Saudi Arabia, it looked as though war might break out. I prayed intently for peace and justice, reminding God that Psalm 46:9 says, *He makes wars cease to the end of the earth,* and in Isaiah 55:11 he said, *So shall my word be that goes out from my mouth; it shall not return to me empty, but it shall accomplish that which I purpose, and succeed in the thing for which I sent it.*

I claimed these two Scriptures and asked God to follow through, but then was reminded by God that humans have free will and God will not take this from them. So I asked forgiveness for my presumption and proceeded to pray for the innocent people caught up in it.

September 7, 1990 —

The Lord has been sending a signal to pray all day. I suspect this is in behalf of Elizabeth and her family who are in Kuwait now and surely must be trying to get out. She is the daughter of a friend, married to an Egyptian citizen, now living in Kuwait, along with their children.

September 16, 1990 —

Many days the Lord has sent trembling lips indicating I should pray. Today he sent powerful jerks and spasms to my lips and I have prayed earnestly all day. [I found out the next day that Elizabeth and her family were leaving Kuwait— making their preparations, standing in lines and waiting on buses and planes. No doubt they were in grave danger but, praises to God, they have made it out to London and are safe.]

September 23, 1990 —

The Lord has been so close lately. I scarcely have thoughts without his sending some hymn to explain or clarify or reinforce the thought. It is so wonderful to know he is following closely what I do and think.

Last night I asked the Lord to come. Early this morning I awakened to see a vapor approaching me. From my perspective I could see *a face appear,* as though it were *a black-and-white photographic negative in three dimensions.* I could even see the eyes. It came closer and closer, then entered my head. At that point my head felt the tingly electric feeling and I heard the noise of the Holy Spirit from the realm of heaven audibly. This is a far-off roar of voices and songs. What wondrous ways the Ruler of the Universe is making himself known to me.

September 25, 1990—

At the Bible study class today I went up for prayer and received the following prophecy. "You are delivered from fear. You are free from it. You will continue in your plans." The teacher took my hands, blessed them and said, "With these hands, you will deliver many to my kingdom. Your dreams of bringing many people to salvation will come true." Praise God! I felt the presence of the Holy Spirit mightily and would have fallen in the power of the Spirit if others hadn't held me up.

An interesting side effect to intense prayer and the presence of the Holy Spirit is actually to feel the flickering of the flames of the Spirit in my mouth or nose or eyes. One day I felt the flickering in the back of my left nostril, another day I felt it in the back of my throat after reciting some Psalms from memory.

November 4, 1990—

What delightful days we have had this past month. Much time has been spent outside, puttering around the yard, digging, planting and just enjoying the Indian Summer weather the Lord has sent. Our tuberous begonias, which suffered during the heat of summer, started thriving and blooming beautifully this past month. Some rain has come but the lake water supply is still low.

Howard bought a pink dogwood tree for my birthday and we will enjoy its blooms next spring. My vegetable garden failed because the woodchucks ate everything. One unfortunate woodchuck was killed on the street going down the hill about a month back. He could have been ours, for we haven't seen one since. I am sorry, for they lived here first and I do not need a garden.

November 9, 1990–

Today I heard and saw geese going over very high. There were great lines of them—several hundred—and they continued to fly over during much of the early evening. How calming is this orderly procession of seasons represented in the movement of birds in migration.

December 15, 1990–

During the night the Lord sent a message while I was feeling the tingling of the Holy Spirit. As I remember it, the Lord said, "Don't be afraid. I am with you all the time to protect you. Lean on me. Let me have all your problems and I will deal with them. You don't have to worry about them. You will finish the book you are writing for me." Praise God!

January 8, 1991–

I was not prepared for last night's prophecy. But how does one prepare for a Word from God that *shatters the status quo of the whole world?* How can one ever be ready to receive a word that loosens every bolt of society, unravels all preconceived notions of history, upsets every future plan of all institutions of business, education, government, religion and family. Even at that, the ramifications of this "word" from God have not even begun to be defined.

In the night God awakened me with the second of what I later discovered would be three prophecies and said to me, *"The last decade."* Accompanying this was the presence of the Holy Spirit as a powerful quivering of my entire body. I sat up in bed and said the phrase over and over again. At the same time I asked the Lord what it meant, yet I realized in my deepest being that *I knew what it meant.* It fills out the puzzle completely—it is the missing last piece.

The Lord has been preparing me for this prophecy for the past seven years. Spiritually I was a creeping, milk-fed baby reaching out in need and desperation. He has lifted me and taught me and chastised me. He has guided my way in the study of his Word; sent message after message of Biblical truths; performed miracles repeatedly in my sight; and tested and tried me in many ways. After I grew in faith and commitment under his tutelage, he began to send messages and visions about the end of the world; he has guided my footsteps and directed my path in many ways even unknown to me.

He has given me the gift of prophecy and directed me to study Revelation and then has shown me countless visions of confirmation of the Book of Revelation; he has sanctified and elevated me to live behind the veil in the "holy of holies" and shown me the fire and cloud of Moses, the whirling wheels, the four living creatures of Ezekiel and Revelation and the symbolic Lamb of God in the Gospel of John.

The Lord has enacted the story of Noah before me in pictures and the story of Hezekiah in flesh; he allowed me to see the angels he sent for protection and ordained me to hear a great battle between good and evil and see the evil one himself in a vision; and he enabled me to see Methuselah, the oldest person who ever lived. He has sent visions, sounds and smells of heaven; he has given me glimpses of the great and powerful light of the living God, his throne, the rainbow colors around him and the magnificent sea of cut glass crystal before him.

At night the Lord has played the story of Jesus before my eyes; showing me the robe of Jesus as well as his face in a pencil sketch. One autumn day, he even allowed me to see the living Christ on a city street. Now the Lord of the Universe is ready for the culmination of all things; he has prophesied the same to a weak mortal like me.

But who will believe this? Even Jesus said, *"But about that day and hour no one knows, neither the angels of heaven, nor the Son, but only the Father"* (Mt 24:36). Then I realized it says "day and hour," not year or decade.

Isaiah 42:9 says, *"See, the former things have come to pass, and new things I now declare; before they spring forth, I tell you of them."* Also in John 16:13 Christ says, *"When the Spirit of truth comes, he will guide you into all the truth; for he will not speak on his own, but will speak whatever he hears, and he will declare to you the things that are to come."*

This is the reason for the book he asked me to write—a way to follow step-by-step and year-by-year—and why he has forbidden me to participate in activities which would compromise sanctification and repeatedly has called me to obedience. I asked the Lord to confirm the message and this morning the Bible opened to the Gospel of John, first page—the story of John the Baptist being called to announce the coming of the Messiah.

January 9, 1991 —

This morning another confirmation came of his message "The last decade" from Isaiah 61:1-2: *The spirit of the Lord God is upon me, because the Lord has anointed me ... to proclaim the year of the Lord's favor, and the day of vengeance of our God.*

I am still wondering how this message will be received. My mind started working on alternatives to the end of the world. I wondered if it might be a warning to America to straighten up and repent or be destroyed. A warning of this type might just be believed. But no. I had hardly considered this possibility when the Lord told me to open the Bible and it opened to Zephaniah 1:1-3: *The word of the Lord that came to Zephaniah son of Cushi son of Gedaliah son of Amariah son of Hezekiah, in the days of King Josiah son of Amon of Judah. I will utterly sweep away everything from the face of the earth, says the Lord. I will sweep away humans and animals; I will sweep away the birds of the air and the fish of the sea. I will make the wicked stumble. I will cut off humanity from the face of the earth, says the Lord.*

January 10, 1991 —

The Lord came to me this morning in wave after wave of euphoria. Last night I sat up a long time talking to God and thinking about his message. I told him I needed to hear the message repeatedly for confirmation so this morning the Bible opened by chance to Joel 3 which contains a description of the end times when all nations are judged: *Let the nations rouse themselves and come up to the valley of Jehoshaphat; for there I will sit to judge all the neighboring nations. Put in the sickle, for the harvest is ripe. Go in, tread, for the wine press is full. The vats overflow, for their wickedness is great. Multitudes, multitudes in the valley of decision! For the day of the Lord is near in the valley of decision. The sun and moon are darkened, and the stars withdraw their shining. The Lord roars from Zion, and utters his voice from Jerusalem, and the heavens and the earth shake. But the Lord is a refuge for his people, a stronghold for the people of Israel* (12-16). Writing this my lips are trembling and my insides shaking with the power of the indwelling Holy Spirit.

January 14, 1991—

The vision of the whirling wheels was repeated last night, but *the wheels finally stopped whirling* and on the end of every spoke I saw *an eye!* Previously I had asked God where were the eyes reported in Ezekiel.

January 27, 1991—

A few days ago I realized the actual purpose of the Roman Catholic rosary. Somewhere I saw a man with a rosary and it came to me that repeating the prayers of the rosary brings the same benefits to a person as repeating memorized Psalms and other Scriptures. It is a healing balm for body, soul and spirit.

February 6, 1991—

While walking up our hill, I stopped to praise God as I used to before we moved to the top of the hill. Just then the wispy mare's tail clouds that were skimming across the sky assembled themselves into the shape of an angel in flight directly above me. It had a face also. Praise God! This, no doubt, was sent by the Lord as a symbol of the presence of his hovering, protecting angels at all times and in all places.

February 10, 1991—

Last March 23 the Lord revealed through a prophecy to Miriam that something I am involved in has three parts. Since we didn't know the meaning, we laid it aside temporarily. Miriam reported last night the Lord told her, "One more." She wondered what it meant. During a time of prayer and meditation I heard the Holy Spirit say the message was for me. The three parts were three prophecies to be revealed to me. The message "one more" meant another one was to come. The first was on Christmas 1989 when the Lord said, "Don't celebrate Christmas." The second was a month ago when the Lord said, "The last decade." I wonder what the third will be.

February 15, 1991—

Surprisingly I did not have to wait several months for the third prophecy arrived this morning, five weeks after the second. It is: *"The Lord is at hand,"* and comes from Philippians 4:5. *The Bible Knowledge Commentary,* by Walvoord and Zuck says, "This probably refers to the rapture, not to his presence with his own at all times." This makes sense and reinforces the second prophecy, "The last decade." Of course, Jesus will return and call his own away before the destruction of the earth. This is the comfort of these prophecies. The third prophecy, therefore, was sent as an assurance of our escape from the terror of world's end.

The Lord sent a confirmation of the third prophecy this evening. While I was out, Howard started playing a record he had not played for months: "Rejoice in the Lord Alway," by Henry Purcell. As I was coming in the room, I heard the choir sing, *"The Lord is at hand; the Lord is at hand."*

How is it, I wonder, that the Lord has honored me by putting in my mouth his divine word? This morning the Bible opened to 2 Timothy 1:9: *[God] who saved us and called us with a holy calling, not according to our works but according to his own purpose and grace. This grace was given to us in Christ Jesus before the ages began.*

Paul adds a few verses later: *And for this reason I suffer as I do. But I am not ashamed, for I know the one in whom I have put my trust, and I am sure that he is able to guard until that day what I have entrusted to him* (v. 12).

Since the Lord sent the message "The last decade," I have been thinking a great deal about this gem of the universe we call earth. What will it be like when time is called? How tall will our newly planted pin oak tree be in ten years? Will there still be warblers migrating across our mountain? Will the sky still be blue and the grass green? Will the air on our mountain still smell sweet and fresh? What will our friends and relatives be doing? How will our goddaughter look at 13? How sad it will be for people who have striven all their lives for money or power or acclaim and have never stopped to see a sunset or swing a child or write a poem. According to Matthew 24 people will be buying and selling, marrying and giving in marriage, giving birth and burying, and few will be looking for the return of the Lord.

I have been inwardly grieving over the destruction of earth because I love it so. Then, the Lord pointed out in Revelation 21: *Then I saw a new heaven and a new earth; for the first heaven and the first earth had passed away, and the sea was no more. And I saw the holy city, the new Jerusalem coming down out of heaven from God, prepared as a bride adorned for her husband. And I heard a loud voice from the throne saying, "See, the home of God is among mortals. He will dwell with them as their God; they will be his peoples, and God himself will be with them; he will wipe every tear from their eyes. Death will be no more; mourning and crying and pain will be no more, for the first things have passed away." And the one who was seated on the throne said, "See, I am making all things new," Also he said, "Write this, for these words are trustworthy and true." Then he said to me, "It is done! I am the Alpha and the Omega, the beginning and the end. To the thirsty I will give water as a gift from the spring of the water of life. Those who conquer will inherit these things, and I will be their God and they will be my children"* (vv. 1-7).

Hurrah! This is it! God will give us a new earth—a perfect earth preserved for his people and we will live with him forever. *Praise be to God: the Father, Son and Holy Spirit!*

Epilogue ✑

[Several significant messages have come since the book ended that add reinforcement to God's revelations contained here.]

March 26, 1991—

Being concerned about the drought we are experiencing and the approach of the tribulation, I have asked the Lord to send rain and received the message from Scripture that Jerusalem is being punished; i.e., the nations are being punished.

Last night the Lord sent a vision of green grass and trees being overtaken by a brown lifeless wave. I thought it was a vision sent by the evil one so I ordered evil out in the name of Jesus and called on the name of the Lord. But the vision did not disappear. Jewels formed at the edges to show that it came from God! The brown wave kept overtaking the green grass until it drew very near to us, then stopped. We were still surrounded by green. Then that vision faded and I saw roots of trees and grasses in the ground which were wet with water that seemed to come from underground. I shuddered at this vivid depiction of a segment of the tribulation.

Later I wondered if the vision were a prediction of a drought of water or of spirit. For the people who have neither sought God nor cared to seek, it surely must be a warning of coming catastrophe. This also reminded me of a warning by Janet's son Eddie who in a near-death experience not long ago saw the glories of heaven, felt the love of Jesus surround him and actually saw the Lord. He said, "God is angry and he says to get ready. *He says you'd better be ready!*"

June 10,1991 –

When I walked in the chapel this morning to pray with the women, Janet was reading a passage which God had opened for her just as she arrived—Acts 17:30-31 which is part of Paul's sermon on Mars Hill to unbelievers: *"While God has overlooked the times of human ignorance, now he commands all people everywhere to repent, because he has fixed a day on which he will have the world judged in righteousness by a man whom he has appointed, and of this he has given assurance to all by raising him from the dead."*

August 1991 –

It is mid-summer as I sit in the family room of our house on the hill. A glance to the south yard fills my vision with marigolds, phlox and geraniums—God's gracious color panorama of the growing season. The view to the west overlooks a river valley with fields of alfalfa and milo tucked in between groves of trees, like moss-green lakes in the middle of a northern forest. It is quiet except for the twittering of hummingbirds and chickadees at the bird feeders. A cool front has arrived and the windows are open. The comforting peace of the Holy Spirit surrounds me; I am afraid of nothing.

The past seven years have brought spiritual growth to me that was unimaginable during my early years. Now I am content with the assurance of God's presence and in whatever future he plans for me. Thinking back to the prophecies God gave me, I realize there are questions yet to be answered. But for those who have given their lives to Jesus, there is nothing to fear. His imminent return will be glorious and fulfilling and our lives will emerge in a climax of unending joy.

Dottie Mae Goard grew up on a Missouri dairy farm near Springfield. She earned a bachelor's degree in chemistry from Southwest Missouri State University and worked as an analytical chemist for Phillips Petroleum Company in Bartlesville, Oklahoma, where she met and married Howard Goard, a chemical engineer from Ohio.

Together they spent many vacations bird watching from Alaska to Mexico and from Washington state to the Florida Keys. She received the Oklahoma Ornithological Society Conservation award for achievements in the education of children in conservation and bird study.

Both Dottie and Howard were active in the First United Methodist church until Howard's death in 1992. Dottie continues as a member of the Evangelism Committee, the Sanctuary Choir, as president of the church retirees' Extra Years of Zest club and the daily prayer team.

She is a certified Lay Speaker for the United Methodist Church, a published poet, a gospel song leader in the local nursing homes and an active volunteer for the Lighthouse Outreach home for the homeless.

Additional copies of this book may be obtained
from your local bookstore
or by sending $13.95 per copy, postpaid

to:

Hope Publishing House
P.O. Box 60008
Pasadena, CA 91116

CA residents kindly add 8¼% tax
FAX orders to (818) 792-2121
VISA/MC orders to (800) 326-2671